D0379771

What About Me?

Strategies for Teaching Misunderstood Learners

Christopher Lee & Rosemary Jackson

HEINEMANN
Portsmouth, NH

Heinemann
A division of Reed Elsevier Inc.
361 Hanover Street
Portsmouth, NH 03801-3912
www.heinemann.com

Offices and agents throughout the world

©2001 by Christopher M. Lee and Rosemary F. Jackson

All rights reserved. No part of this book may be reproduced in any form or by any electronic or mechanical means, including information storage and retrieval systems, without permission in writing from the publisher, except by a reviewer, who may quote brief passages in a review.

Library of Congress Cataloging-in-Publication Data
Lee, Christopher M.
    What about me?: strategies for teaching misunderstood learners / Christopher Lee, Rosemary Jackson.
        p. cm.
    Includes bibliographical references.
    ISBN 0-325-00348-3
        1. Learning disabled children—Education—United States—Case studies. 2. Learning disabled—United States—Bibliography. 3. Lee, Christopher M. I. Jackson, Rosemary F. II. Title.

LC4705. L443 2000
371.9'0973—dc21   00-046088

Editor: William Varner
Production service: Colophon
Production coordinator: Lynne Reed
Cover design: Jenny Jensen Greenleaf
Manufacturing: Deanna Richardson

Printed in the United States of America on acid-free paper
05   04   03   02   01   DA   1   2   3   4   5

My Teacher, Sister Ann

I stared hard at the blackboard, with a blank expression. I could feel all eyes on me as I strained to recognize and read aloud the word on the board. Her voice got stronger as she repeated my name over and over: "Christopher? Christopher? Christopher?" I heard her but did not answer—could not answer. I had pulled into my own world, a world that offered me safety. Sister Ann did not give up. She continued to call my name and slowly moved closer to me. The tone of her voice had changed. No longer was she demanding that I answer her. Now she was more concerned to know if I was OK. The murmurs of my seventh grade classmates got louder as Sister Ann bent down and touched my arm. I was nowhere to be found. Nothing could hurt me now—I was oblivious to all outside stimuli. The world had become a very small place—a place where I did not fit in, a place that I did not belong. As space rejects humans by depriving them of oxygen, so Planet Earth was rejecting me because of my inability to communicate effectively.

I was an alien among my peers. And everyone knew—except Sister Ann.

My attention focused on Sister Ann. Strong and quiet, she had a way of presiding intensely over the class. Her lessons flowed off her tongue, bringing understanding to her students year after year. Teaching was her passion and gift, and I was fortunate to have her as my teacher. Why could I not learn like everyone else in the class? How is it that I could not "get" what was presented right in front of me? Sister Ann tried so hard to work with me and to help me understand her lessons.

I could see that the other students "got it." I watched it day after day in each of their eyes as the material was taken in and comprehended—eager baby birds waiting to be fed. Then there was me. I was always in the back of the nest, letting everyone else take in what they needed in order to survive and feeding off the leftovers. Even though I could see in Sister Ann's eyes that she liked me, I did not feel it!

As I look back at that time in my life, I realize the amazing commitment that Sister Ann gave to me and all her students on a daily basis. Her determination and passion for teaching ran through her veins. She lived, breathed, and loved her gift of teaching. I was fortunate to know her. I remember inviting her to my seventh grade birthday party, to which she came. I should not have been surprised when I unwrapped her gift to find a math book. Puzzled then, touched now, I understand the larger gift she gave me: her belief and commitment to me. She made a difference in my life at a very difficult time.

For Sister Ann and all the other teachers out there who are able to give not only the gift of education, but also the gift of hope to their students, I thank you and dedicate this book to you. You should feel proud of the profession you have chosen. You are needed, and you impact the lives of your students more than you'll ever know. Thank you for striving to be the best no matter what hurdles you may face. Your time is far from wasted.

Contents

Preface

*W*hen Rosemary and I started writing our first book, *Faking It: A Look Into the Mind of a Creative Learner,* I was only 21 years old and extremely naive. My ignorance about the field of learning disabilities (LD) flowed out of every word I wrote. I knew little about labels, definitions, laws, or even my own individual learning disabilities. Like the parable of the blind men who went to "see" an elephant for the first time, I had many misconceptions of what a learning disability actually was. LD specialists tried to explain to me that I had a "cognitive processing deficit," which affected the way my brain dealt with information. All I knew for sure was that my brain would reject anything that dealt with academics. However, I did not know the extent of how this processing problem would affect my everyday life and the jobs I would hold. Like the blind men who visited the elephant, my disability changed perspectives depending on the challenges I encountered each day.

Another piece of the picture that kept slipping through my fingers was the importance of putting myself in the right place, whether with the right teacher, the right job, or the right mentors. I did not understand that these selections could make the difference between success and failure.

As I dictated page after page of that first book, I worked through the anger that I had stored up for so many years. In *Faking It,* I offered a naive interpretation of what I believed was going on inside of me. Because I had no professional training, I spoke with a raw passion, honesty, and clarity drawn from my personal, often painful experiences, as an individual with a disability. Over the last few years, as I have evolved into a professional, there are times when I feel I have misplaced that *innocent* clarity of vision.

This book reflects the growth in my professional knowledge. I have listened to and learned from many professionals in the field. The more knowledge I gained, the hazier things became. Professionals explain things differently; they each seem to have their own individual way of visualizing this complex disorder. I feel that the common threads among different researchers are even more obscured because of the competition among professionals to publish and to be heard the loudest in their fields. At times it seemed to me that there were a multitude of theories and few solutions. Listening to theory after theory, I took in every word I could. Although I had been exposed to some of the most brilliant people in the field, my frustration started simmering just as it had when I was writing about my classroom struggles with the education system in *Faking It*. I even found myself caught up in the net. *Collaboration* seemed to be another word for a mutual admiration society.

As I was struggling to find my way as a professional, Rosemary was questioning her own goals in life. Having worked for many years in a clinical environment, she decided it was time to return to her first love—teaching. When a job opened in the special education department of her small hometown college, she knew she wanted to enter the field of teacher education. We continued to collaborate through the years, this time as professionals working together to find answers for all the students who were struggling through the education system.

This book is very different from *Faking It*. I now speak from the perspective of a person with a learning disability who is also an advocate in the field. I am a consumer of services while, at the same time, serving other consumers. *What About Me?* is for all the misunderstood learners who are searching for strategies that will help them succeed. It is for the teachers and parents who put themselves out there everyday to help these students. Through insight and experience, Rosemary and I will share with you strategies to help guide you through the mind of the misunderstood learner.

This book is written through a unique collaborative effort. Through dictation, my voice is carried to Rosemary's fingertips. A majority of the time, this book offers my direct perspective through personal stories and experiences. At other times, the book combines the voices of both of us, offering the unique insight of a dual perspective. *What About Me?* is a testimony of how a collaborative-writing team approach can be successful. Writing this book has not only given us the opportunity to explore and research misunderstood learners, but more importantly, it has allowed us to have time together, remembering classroom stories and sharing old times. We hope you enjoy reading this book as much as we enjoyed writing it.

Acknowledgments

This book is made up of many voices. They lent emotional support, personal stories, unique insight, helpful strategies, and even the fun research stuff. This book is not about *What About Me?* It is a story of many people—a story of individuals with learning disabilities, friends, family members, teachers, and colleagues all coming together through my and Rosemary's voices. This book could not have been written without the support of the following individuals and the gifts they gave us:

To the patience of Don Jackson: thank you for sacrificing your already limited time with Rosemary for the good of others. To Kathy and Michael Lee—Mom and Dad—thanks for the gift of Risk Taking. No matter how hard things get, you both are always there for me. I love you for your support and insight. To my family, from which I draw so very much: Nana, Art, K. K., Lester, Craig, Angela, Michelle, Alfred, and my nephews and niece, Stuart, Ben, Ryan, Jacob, and Emily—you are my inspiration. To my colleague, Joy Kniskern, for the time and belief you gave me. To Theresa King ("the syntax queen"), who put up with me when the work load got heavy. Theresa, I could not have handled my work load without your support.

To my dear friend, Carolyn Phillips, for your knowledge, poetry, and love. To my confidant, Dr. Bill Bergeron, for your friendship. To Seam Drakon, for teaching me a valuable lesson about myself that will follow me throughout my life and for inspiring the title of this book, *What About Me?* To Dr. Noel Gregg, who provided me with opportunities and a foundation for growth. To the board of directors of LD Adults of Georgia, for keeping me focused on what this is all about. To Bill Kennedy, for being my friend and co-conspirator. To Helene Johnson, for your support and invaluable ear. To Kendra Lee and Valerie Wiley, for your graphic talents. To Neil Struomski, for your guidance and friendship. To Nancie Payne, for your knowledge and amazing lifetime stories. To my friends Gregg Sams, Doug Neal, Jeff Smith, and Kevin Mylod, for putting up with my obsessive discussions about this book; thanks for letting me bend your ears. Finally, to Marshall Raskind, Richard Wanderman, Kim Hartsell, and the Tools for Life staff, for their resources.

Christopher M. Lee

———

This book would not have been possible without the love and support of my husband, Don, who not only gave me up on weekends, but also supported my and Christopher's endeavors by feeding us homemade biscuits, grits, and red-eye gravy on Saturday mornings. I would also like to acknowledge the support and friendship of Dee Russell and Karynne Kleine, who provided reflective insight into the writing process as well as Christopher's self-analysis, and also provided Don with their friendship and company during my preoccupation with this book. I would also like to acknowledge the support of my department chair, Dr. Craig Smith, and the Dean of the John H. Lounsbury School of Education, Dr. Leslie Crawford.

Rosemary F. Jackson

One

What If?

A mind stretched to accept a new idea can never regain its original dimensions.

— Albert Einstein

Jacob is not quite a year old. With blond hair, blue eyes, he mimics me as I make faces above him. Stretching and wiggling around the crib, Jacob can barely control himself as his active little body responds to the new stimulus leaning over his crib. Taking in this miracle baby, I find myself without breath and pondering whether or not Jacob will grow up with the same struggles and difficulties as his father and I. I ask myself the same question every time I see him: Does Jacob have a learning disability? Will the genetic strand continue to disrupt the next generation, my nephew, Jacob?

When looking at Jacob, I am aware of all the possible gifts that he could bring into this life. However, I can't keep from thinking, What If . . .

He doesn't speak until he is three years old?

He has trouble writing his first letter?
Or reading his first birthday card?

What if Jacob fails the second grade?

What if he gets put into special education and speech classes?

What if he turns 16 and can't pass his drivers license test?

What if he gets caught in an embarrassing situation trying to write his first check?

What if he considers dropping out of high school?

What if he never completes a job application because it is too hard to read or fill out?

What if he grows up to believe he is worthless because he has limited ability to read, write, or remember simple facts—like how to spell his name?

What if Jacob mimics more than my funny looking faces and grows up like me?

Thirty-five percent of students identified as having learning disabilities drop out of high school, contributing greatly to the nation's drop-out rates. Learning disabilities and substance abuse are the most common impediments to keeping welfare recipients from becoming and remaining employed, according to a 1992 report from the Office of the Inspector General. It is estimated that between 50 and 80 percent of students in Adult Basic Education classes have learning disabilities. The number of prison inmates with learning disabilities ranges from 30 to 50 percent (Wagner 1991). In order for Jacob not to fall into this pool of negative statistics, it will take several key components merging together at points throughout his life to ensure smooth transitions and positive outcomes.

Life is made up of a continuance of short-term and long-term goals. The very first, raw, primal goal is established at birth, usually by the parents. They want to ensure—no matter what it takes—that this child will have a happy and fulfilling life.

Baby Jacob has all the love in the world and will hopefully grow up to reach this goal. If Jacob had been born with some type of physical disability, this goal would be tougher to reach. Specific and crucial components would need to be put into place in order for Jacob to fulfill his parents' basic goal. A physical disability is usually obvious from the beginning. The parents automatically begin to readjust their expectations and often become frightened about what the future will hold for their child. If Jacob has been born with a learning disability, several years might pass before his parents begin to realize that Baby Jacob is not meeting their or society's expectations. Dreams will diminish day by day as parents and teachers become complacent with the idea that Baby Jacob will fall short of the primal goal.

After I was evaluated and *found out* (that I had a learning disability) in the second grade, my parents started to readjust their original goal for my life. I am sure that they still believed I would obtain a fulfilling life even though they now had to deal with this "glitch," a temporary problem focused around my academic achievement. I can imagine my dad saying, "Everything will be fine," denial setting in. "Christopher will just have to work harder. If we stay on the teachers' backs, things will work out." My mother, being the patient and practical one in the family, knew something was deeply wrong. She not only realized that I was dealing with difficulties forming letters and reading words, but also sensed that an emotional struggle was beginning to brew deep within her child. As a second grader I remember feeling an emotional conflict within myself. I was different from the other children around me. Thoughts and words did not come easy for me. Language became my adversary. I failed the second grade.

Christopher: 0
Language: 1

It was at this point that my parents' long-term goal—my achieving a happy and fulfilling life—began to be replaced by a series of short-term goals: read this word, pass this test, complete this page of math problems—get out of the second grade so you can start all of this over in the third grade. Every bit of effort and energy on the part of my parents, teachers, and myself was put into small achievable goals that focused on basic remediation. At no time do I ever remember anyone telling me that by learning to read and write, one day I could become President of the United States—or, better yet, the New Millennium version of success: President of Microsoft, Inc. Instead, I began a long journey through the world of special education.

This alien world was then, and still is, a very difficult one to navigate. People in this world at first appear to speak English; however, once one gets beyond the basic introduction phase, you quickly realize these people are speaking a language you have never heard. This is why we are beginning this book with some basic definitions. The purpose of this chapter is to attempt to give parents and general education teachers enough basic knowledge of "how things work" in special education so that they can be active and knowledgeable participants in helping to decide the best course of action for a child with learning disabilities in the public school system. First, let's consider exactly what special education is, and then we will explore the educational environments that are possible placements for students with disabilities.

Special Education is simply specially designed instruction. To be eligible for this special instruction, students are considered according to two standards: categorical and functional. The student must have a confirmed disability (categorical), and the disability must cause a need for specially designed instruction (functional). The categories that fall under the Individuals with Disabilities Education Act (IDEA) are specific learning disabilities; emotional disturbance; mental retardation, including severe and multiple disabilities; autism; other health impairments; orthopedic impairments; traumatic brain injury; speech or language impairments; hearing impairments, including deafness; and visual/blindness impairments (Turnbull et al. 1999).

If students have a confirmed disability that causes a need for specially designed instruction, their needs may be met by school systems in a variety of different ways. A *regular class* is the type of class the majority of students in public schools attend. These classes are typically divided by grades, and students who are in these classes identify themselves as being in that grade. They can easily answer the question, "What grade are you in?" Most of the students in this type of class do not have identified disabilities, although they may encounter difficulty with classroom material from time to time. A strong school curriculum should be challenging even when material is presented "on grade level." Regular classes are taught by "regular" or general education teachers who have extensive knowledge about teaching curriculum appropriate for the age level of their students but who may have little training in how to teach this curriculum to students with disabilities.

A *resource room* is a type of class where students can go for special assistance outside the regular class. Typically, students leave their regular classroom and go to a separate room, which is taught by a teacher who has specialized training. Students generally go to this resource teacher for instruction in those subjects that are most negatively affected by their disabilities. For example, a student with learning disabilities that primarily affect his or her ability to read might attend a resource room for one or two hours a day to receive specialized instruction in reading. Sometimes the student will leave his or her regular classroom at the same time as the other students are getting their reading instruction. In other cases, the student may participate in the regular reading instruction with his or her peers and go to the resource teacher for remediation in specific areas related to reading (e.g., phonological awareness).

A *separate class* is a type of class where students with special needs spend more than 60 percent of their day. These classes are usually referred to as *self-contained classes*. Students in these classes receive the majority of instruction from a special education teacher. They are usually considered by the school system to be special education students rather than students who are in a particular grade. In fact, self-contained special education classes may often contain students from a variety of grades. Often, when you ask a student from a self-contained class, "What grade are you in?" he or she may reply, "I'm in Mrs. Jackson's room."

A *separate school* is sometimes recommended for students with severe types of disabilities. Students who attend a separate day school for more than half of the school day at the public's expense are considered to be placed at a separate school. Some parents choose to remove students from the public school system and have them educated in a private school that specializes in educating students with certain types of disabilities. The advantages and disadvantages of these schools are discussed later in this chapter.

Over the last couple of years, I have become an advocate in the education field. In doing so, I have developed some strong opinions about the education system. Through speaking to parents, teachers, and school systems across the country, I have learned that some states are stronger than others in providing educational services to the disability community. This one point is what makes this chapter so tough to write. There is no general blanket that you can spread over special education to put this problem to rest. I have found that some communities still do everything they possibly can to keep general education students separate from those with special educational needs, while other communities embrace the disability population in their schools. The reason why I feel this chapter is so important is because one of the most frequent questions I am asked is, "Should I put my child in a special education class or keep him in regular education?" My immediate reaction to that question is usually a flinch, followed by a deep breath. I have learned to restrain myself from projecting my personal negative experiences in special education into the parent's question. Times have changed since I was in special education, and I have seen some remarkable teachers doing remarkable things in classrooms around the country. I usually answer this question with ambiguity. There is no way, at this point in my career, that I will feel comfortable giving a definitive answer. The waters are still too muddy, and there are specific questions that I would have to ask in order to give a professional opinion. This chapter is designed to look at some of those questions and to examine the pros and cons of placing a student in regular or special education.

My struggles started in the first grade. I was a failure by the second. Pulled out, I was placed in a separate school, my county's answer to dealing with its population of students with special needs. My journey through special education had begun. I rode a special bus—a smaller bus designed to carry students who use wheelchairs, students who are deaf and blind, and students who look very different from most people, all heading to the same place.

I remember feeling scared and lost. How could my parents take me away from my friends and put me in this place . . . a place that I felt I didn't belong? Unlike the other students on this bus, I could walk and talk and see and hear. As I think back to that time, I'm sure there were other students with labels like mine, but they faded into the background, while the people with physical disabilities were magnified. For the first few months, I felt pity for them. I must have believed I was better than they were because I had capabilities they didn't. From the outside I looked normal and they didn't. Katie always sat in the back of the bus with the other children who used wheelchairs. At first glance, Katie frightened me. She looked so different from the girls I had ridden with the year before. She had light brown hair that was always matted because of the headrest on the wheelchair. She had some movement in her arms, but it was jerky and took much effort. Her speech was slurred at times and missing words, like holes in Swiss cheese. Alice always sat right behind the driver, facing forward, as if she controlled the bus. Throughout our journey to school, Alice would turn her head to look behind at the rest of us. She was the caretaker of the bus. She would scold us for being too loud but was ready to help anyone who needed it. She stood much taller than the rest of us and wore thick red glasses, which, she told me later, prevented the sun from reaching her sensitive eyes. Her skin and hair were white and pasty like Elmer's glue. Robert James, always called by both names, was the only African American on the bus. He was skinny and short, about my size, and always sat in the same seat. He wore thick dark glasses and used a silver stick that he scraped along the ground. I learned to listen for the windshield wiper sound he made as he walked. I remember going home some days and trying to copy Robert James, whittling my own canes from sticks in the woods and trying to find my way back to my house. I was fascinated with Robert James and how he managed to go from the lunchroom to the restroom to the playground without missing a beat.

In the beginning, I was a scared kid. During those first few months of stepping onto that school bus, I truly believed I did not belong. I was not like these kids! However, over the course of a year, things changed. Without realizing it, I began to make friends with each one of these "misplaced" kids. Looking back, my most vivid memories of Katie and Alice and Robert James were not of their disabilities, but of their capabilities. Katie had the ability to connect with people through her sparkling eyes. It's hard to describe, but I felt good being around her. Her eyes gave me truth. Alice showed me how to be strong. Robert James spurred my imagination. By the end of the school year, I was no longer scared of my new friends. By watching them, I knew deep down that they were much smarter than I was, even with their obvious disabilities. I was beginning to figure out why I was a passenger on the little yellow school bus.

The next September rolled around too soon, and before I knew it I was beginning second grade all over in a brand new school. I clearly remember that first day of school. The desk was cold and hard as I slipped quietly into it. The desk was nothing like the soft sand and warm water I played in all summer. This was not a beach, and I was not looking forward to repeating the second grade at this brand new school. Even though I was a year older than the other students around me, I did not feel bigger or smarter. The large room was filled with strangers. My friends were at another school. My eyes kept drifting toward the window in the far corner of the room. It was a small window, but just large enough for me to crawl through, which is exactly what I wanted to do. I quickly noticed that my parents had decided to put me back in with kids that looked like me. No longer were there kids like Katie, Alice, or Robert James. Instead of being in a whole school of kids who didn't fit in, now those of us who were different were simply moved throughout the day to the "Stupid Trailers" behind the school. In these "resource rooms," there were "special" teachers who were supposed to fix my brain with "magical" books, cards, and games. For the next several years, I found myself continuously being pulled out of my regular classes to go not only to the Stupid Trailer, but also to the speech class down the hall. It didn't seem to matter where I went or what class I was in, words and letters and numbers would not stand still or hold their shapes long enough for me to grasp them.

Grade after grade went by. I hated school. I hated myself. By the fifth grade, I was an eleven-year-old boy with an extremely low self-concept. I was a boy who could not learn by traditional methods. Education had not met the challenge of teaching me. My mother continued to work with the school system, attending teacher conferences and arranging tutoring sessions. However, my father went a different route, focusing not on the education system, but on sports. For the first time, I had a glimpse of something positive to pull through that classroom window I always wanted to crawl out of. The sport of swimming became my lifeline. I ended my journey through special education at the end of the ninth grade, when my parents and I decided to move forward rather than remain behind in the special education system. This was the first time I was given an active voice in this important decision. In the back of my mind, I hoped that not having to attend those special education classes meant that I was "fixed." I was still a long way from facing my disability head-on.

Accepting that there is no choice in certain aspects of who I am has been the hardest thing I have ever dealt with. Growing up as an athlete, I have always wanted to be taller and stronger. When I was younger, my father put me on a weight-training program that built muscle mass. However, there was no special program that could make me taller. If there were, I would have found it. It frustrates me that I can control one part of my life but not another. I could control how strong I was through discipline and working out every day with weights, molding my body into what I wanted it to look like. However, no matter how many hours I spent hanging upside down suspended from my closet doorway, I never forced my body to meet my 6'2" ideal. I have learned and accepted that my height is a part of who I am and something over which I have no control (until science invents that Tall Pill). I don't have to like it; I do have to accept it. This statement couldn't be more relevant to how I feel about my learning disabilities. Accepting that there is no choice in certain aspects of who I am has been very difficult.

I believe that if I had been involved from the beginning in the decision-making process related to my special education placements, I might have come to terms with my learning disabilities much sooner. I know that my parents and teachers all thought they were doing what was best for me, but I never understood why I had to go to a special school or to the Stupid Trailers, and no one ever asked for my opinion. Fortunately, things are done differently today. Both students and parents are now encouraged to participate in decisions about where in the school system a student with special needs can best be served. Another change for the better is the developing philosophy that students with disabilities can and should be educated with their peers in the regular classroom. Teachers have found over the years that the strategies used by special educators can also be beneficial to use with students who have no learning difficulties. Using these strategies, along with appropriate accommodations for special needs students, teachers can now teach to a diverse range of students. This concept is called *inclusion*, and there are a variety of models and levels of controversy surrounding this idea.

The concept of inclusion has changed tremendously over the last twenty-five years. In the beginning, with the passage of laws making it illegal to exclude children with disabilities from public education, the concept was called *mainstreaming*. This focused on making sure that all students received the same education as those who had no disabilities and that special education support systems were developed to help these students succeed. I am a product of that time. If the concept of mainstreaming had not come about, it is likely that I would have completed my entire school career in a special school similar to the one I attended in the second grade. As it was, I became a vital part of the transition era; I was a guinea pig for all the experimental methods being tried out during the 1970s.

The issue of whether or not students with disabilities should be educated within the general education classroom or within specialized settings within the schools has been debated since those early years. Parents and teachers who hated to see their children and students struggle with a general curriculum often argued for long-term placements in special education classrooms. Special education teachers, who often feel they are better trained to help these students than are general education teachers, also argue for keeping students in their classes for as long as possible for specialized instruction. Some people fear that special education support systems currently in the schools may be dismantled if total inclusion continues to be pushed. Adding confusion to the matter is the fact that some schools that have implemented inclusion have experienced negative reactions from teachers, parents, and administrators. In these situations, the schools often declared inclusion to be a failure and went back to a traditional program after a year. This is hardly time to work out the "kinks."

Many inclusion attempts have been successful, and recent research indicates that students with mild disabilities in some models have made significantly greater gains than students in resource programs in the subject areas of reading and language arts (Madden et al. 1993; Jenkins et al. 1994) as well as significantly greater gains in reading, writing, and math (Manset and Semmel 1997; Schulte, Osborne, and McKinney 1990). Most studies have concentrated on inclusion from teachers' perspectives. A comprehensive study by Scruggs and Mastropieri (1996) indicates that teachers feel strongly that, for inclusion to be successful, they must be given additional planning time and training, as well as more professional help in the classroom, additional resource material that is appropriate for the

11

students with disabilities, and a reduction in class size to fewer than twenty students. The most successful inclusion programs appear to be those where entire schools adopt the concept of inclusion and restructure their schools for the benefit of all students. These schools develop a culture wherein teaching for diversity is emphasized over teaching for the "norm." A very successful approach in these schools seems to be cooperative teaching, which provides special education within general education classroom environments. Typically, cooperative teaching involves two or more educators sharing the responsibility for planning and evaluating instruction for students (Thousand, Villa, and Nevin 1994; Bauwens and Hourcade 1995). Cooperative teaching reduces the need for pull-out programs because more individualization takes place in the general education classrooms. If done well, this model also benefits students without exceptionalities, because they benefit from individualized instruction.

Few research studies are available concerning this new concept of inclusion; however, a comprehensive study of seven hundred general and special education teachers and administrators from five states and one Canadian province views cooperative teaching very favorably. This study, by Villa et al. (1996), found that in schools using this model both general and special educators shared responsibility for meeting the needs of all children and were able to work together as co-equal partners; the team teaching resulted in enhanced feelings of competency for both the general and special education students. The progress of students in this study was not compared to students in other special education placements; however, the students with exceptionalities did not lose ground by being placed full time in general education classes; their achievement levels did not decrease.

My perfect classroom setting would involve inclusion and collaboration. There would be two teachers per classroom. This teaching team would be made up of one special education teacher and one general education teacher. I can picture a large classroom with natural lighting coming in from the roof. The room would feel warm and inviting. The classroom would be ergonomically furnished—chairs and desks would be exactly the right proportion for each individual student. While being comfortable, the chairs would be designed to prevent lounging. Group brainstorming tables would be strategically placed around the classroom. The classroom would be a laptop classroom. Each student would be provided with his or her own personal laptop with hardware and software to meet the individual needs of each student. For example, someone who has visual impairments or reading disabilities would have a Screen Reader with headphones. Someone with eye–hand coordination problems might use a key guard placed over his or her keyboard to promote accuracy in typing. Because laptops are portable, students would be able to move them from class to class easily, as well as take them home. This will build responsibility in the children.

Classroom instruction would be provided in a multisensory format, which includes visual, auditory, and kinesthetic teaching. Peer teaching would also be a large part of daily instruction. I envision having older students come in to work with small groups of younger students as facilitators around the brainstorming tables. Peer teaching would make the older students feel responsible, and the younger students might feel more comfortable and try harder. Classroom topics would revolve around long-term popular themes (e.g., Olympics, Wars, Stars, Star Wars, etc.) that could be easily visualized by the students and promote easy discussion and interaction. The school day would not be broken into individual subject areas, allowing longer periods of time for students to explore thematic activities. Specific skill development activities would be incorporated into the themes and designed to help students relate the skills to everyday life activities. Research (Turnbull et al. 1999) has shown that one of the best means of teaching specific skills is to use short periods of intense instruction.

Having two teachers in the room would allow both group and individualized instruction. The students would have a diverse range of abilities. I would like to think that teachers would spend time at the beginning of each school year analyzing each student's strengths, weaknesses, and individual social/emotional needs, and placing them in classroom environments that best fit these qualities.

In my actual experience in the educational system, the best model I encountered was at the University of Georgia. This model allowed me to attend my daily classes just like everyone else and sign up for individual tutoring from an LD specialist (although it would have been nice to actually have the two teachers in the classroom while I was learning the material). Another reason why this model worked so well for me was the open communication with my professors. The LD Center knew the professors well enough to advise me about which ones would be a good match for my learning style. Through self-advocacy training and role playing at the Center, I learned how to disclose my disability and ask for accommodations in a positive way at the beginning of every quarter. I took most of my tests at the Center, with extended time and a reader. The intense tutoring taught me the specific strategies I needed to conquer the material for each course I took. There was also a proactive push to use assistive technology, which opened a new world for me. Peer support groups were also offered, although I wasn't ready to take advantage of them at that time. I don't see why components of this model can't be used in a high school setting, or even with younger students. All we need to do is get rid of all the red tape!

———————

There are two components to take into account when considering the appropriate placement for a student with learning disabilities: the student and the design of the program. Every student has individual needs, and every program operates in its own individual manner. The goal is to get the right match between the student and the program. We cannot emphasize enough how important it is for the student to be involved in the decision-making process from the very beginning. When the student, his or her parents, teachers, and other school officials are gathered together as a decision-making team, the following elements should be considered.

1. The Student's Learning Profile

In order to make appropriate decisions regarding the type of program that best fits a student's needs, it is very important to have a clear idea of the student's learning profile. For example, students who learn best by listening will learn better from a teacher who presents information in a highly verbal context, while students who learn best with visual illustrations need to be in learning environments that make heavy use of graphic organizers, videotapes, movies, pictures, computer graphics, and other such visual illustrations. Students who need to move around in order to learn need to be in environments that are organized to allow activity, while students who have difficulty providing their own structure may work best in an environment that is highly structured and organized. Because I am a kinesthetic learner, I need an environment that provides me room to move around. I never realized how helpful movement was to learning, because I never experienced such a setting until I was an adult.

2. Age

The age of the student should be a major consideration in placement decisions. Students who are identified at a very early age can benefit from specialized instruction, so longer specialized instructional periods may need to be considered. Students who are not identified until they are older, however, risk damage to their self-esteem if they are suddenly removed from their classmates. A better choice for older students might be additional remediation after school. Sometimes parents spend lots of time and energy fighting the school system and/or fighting the disability rather than reframing it into something that's positive. Open communication among parents, teachers, and children is essential. This communication should be at the level best suited to the age of the child.

3. Self-esteem

If the student has strong self-esteem and is involved in an activity such as sports or music, more risks can be taken in considering the special education environment. It is important that adolescents have control over the choices being offered, even though those choices might not be the best ones in the minds of parents and teachers. If the student has low self-esteem, it is important that the decision-making team discuss suggestions for developing outside interests in which the student can find success. Self-esteem is the base of academic success and should be addressed in every academic planning meeting (see Chapter Seven for further discussion).

4. Friends

Research indicates that students with severe disabilities often have more friendships in general education settings than they do in separate settings (Hunt et al. 1994; Staub et al. 1994; Hunt et al. 1996; Turnbull et al. 1999). Other studies on inclusion also indicate that classmates without disabilities experience positive outcomes when students with severe disabilities are included in their classes (Giangreco et al. 1993; Hollowood et al. 1994; Sharpe, York, and Knight 1994). In the last few years, I have found it interesting that when I disclose my disability to my friends, using the word *dyslexia* instead of the term *learning disabilities*, they are fascinated with my story. At times, I feel unique in a positive way. I refrain from going into details about my disabilities and just answer the questions they ask. Growing up, I had difficulty making friends because of my own self-esteem issues. It wasn't until I got involved in an outside activity away from school that I started to develop close, meaningful friendships. Students with learning disabilities may need assistance in developing the specific skills needed to maintain friendships, and these skills should be considered when developing long-term educational plans.

5. *Counseling*

When I think of counseling students with learning disabilities, I relate to two types of counseling procedures: individual and group. Writing *Faking It* was the first time I really started addressing the anger I had with the education system, my parents, and myself. Being a perfectionist, or what I consider an A-type personality, I found myself always pushing to be perfect—and, of course, always falling short. I started individual counseling after I finished *Faking It*. I needed to address issues of self-esteem and self-worth that I had repressed from a very early age. Individual counseling served as a vehicle to undo most of the negative feelings I had about myself. I found it helpful to find a counselor who had experience with disability issues. She would "call" me on the "victim" that continually came out during our sessions. It took several years before The Victim packed his bags and left. The second type of counseling that is effective for people with disabilities is group peer therapy. Basically, this is a support group for individuals with learning disabilities. Usually, these types of support groups are difficult to keep going. I can only assume from my own personal experiences that it is much easier to "fake it" than to confront difficult personal issues. I recommend both types of therapy, particularly if the facilitator has an understanding of disabilities. Counseling concerns need to be considered during educational planning meetings. Evidence of emotional turmoil in a child, which could involve anger, complacency, perfectionism, giving up easily, crying, or behavior problems, should send up a red flag that counseling intervention needs to take place.

6. *Transition Elements*

Special education law requires that transition be formally addressed when a child is fourteen. However, I believe there are elements of transition that need to be considered throughout a child's life. Students with learning disabilities need more specific long-range planning. I think a transition plan should be a working document that follows a child throughout his or her career. Both long-term and short-term goals need to be considered. Transition statements need to be included in the first educational plan ever written. For students at young ages, the transition statements would be exploratory. Parents and students may explore different opportunities for developing outside interests, which may become a positive part of the students' lives. As students get older, transition statements may involve the exploration of actual job opportunities in their communities. Parents or teachers may be able to obtain permission for a student to spend a day shadowing someone on a job. The more focused a student becomes on his or her long-range transition goals, the more effective he or she will be in developing an official transition plan at age fourteen.

Another element of transition that needs to be addressed is transition from school to school, and possibly from grade to grade. It would have helped ease some of the negative feelings I had about moving to another grade or school if I had had the opportunity to meet the teachers or if I could have taken a tour of the school. Educational plans need to incorporate specific steps designed to ease this transition and build students' excitement levels. Visiting a pep rally or attending a football game could make the transition to high school much easier. Instead of students being overwhelmed at the beginning of transitions, they would go in with positive attitudes, because they would know exactly where their rooms are located and would have met their teachers.

In summary, students with learning disabilities, their parents, and their teachers all need to learn the basic skills necessary to navigate in the world of special education so that they can be active and knowledgeable participants in the life-long decision-making process for these individuals who are often misunderstood simply because they experience the world in a different way from most of us.

Works Cited

Bauwens, J., and J. J. Hourcade. 1995. *Cooperative Teaching: Rebuilding the Schoolhouse for All Students.* Austin, TX: Pro-Ed.

Giangreco, M., S. Edelman, R. Dennis, and C. Cloninger. 1993. "My Child Has a Classmate with Severe Disabilities: What Parents of Nondisabled Children Think About Full Inclusion." *Developmental Disabilities Bulletin* 21 (1): 77–91.

Hollowood, T. M., C. L Salisbury, B. Rainforth, and M. M. Palombaro. 1994. "Use of Instructional Time in Classrooms Serving Students with and Without Severe Disabilities." *Exceptional Children* 61: 242–53.

Hunt, P., M. Alwell, F. Farron-Davis, and L. Goetz. 1996. "Creating Socially Supportive Environments for Fully Included Students Who Experience Multiple Disabilities." *Journal of the Association for Persons with Severe Handicaps* 21 (2): 53–71.

Hunt, P., F. Farron-Davis, S. Beckstead, D. Curtis, and L. Goetz. 1994. "Evaluating the Effects of Placement of Students with Severe Disabilities in General Education Versus Special Classes." *Journal of the Association for Persons with Severe Handicaps* 19: 200–14.

Jenkins, J. R., M. Jewell, N. Leichester, R. E. O'Connor, L. M. Jenkins, and N. M. Troutner. 1994. "Accommodations for Individual Differences Without Classroom Ability Groups: An Experiment in School Restructuring." *Exceptional Children* 60: 344–58.

Madden, N. A., R. E. Slavin, N. L. Karweit, L. J. Dolan, and B. A. Wasik. 1993. "Success for All: Longitudinal Effects of a Restructuring Program for Inner-City Elementary Schools." *American Educational Research Journal* 30: 123–48.

Manset, G., and M. I. Semmell. 1997. "Are Inclusive Programs for Students with Mild Disabilities Effective? A Comparative Review of Model Programs." *The Journal of Special Education* 31: 155–80.

Office of the Inspector General, Department of Health and Human Resources. 1992. *Functional Impairments of AFDC Clients*. Washington, D. C.: U. S. Government Printing Office.

Schulte, A. C., S. S. Osborne, and J. D. McKinney. 1990. "Academic Outcomes for Students with Learning Disabilities in Consultation and Resource Programs." *Exceptional Children* 57: 162–72.

Scruggs, T. E., and M. Mastropieri. 1996. "Teacher Perceptions of Mainstreaming/Inclusion, 1958–1995: A Research Synthesis." *Exceptional Children* 63: 59–74.

Sharpe, M. N., J. L. York, and J. Knight. 1994. "Effects of Inclusion on the Academic Performance of Classmates Without Disabilities: A Preliminary Study." *Remedial and Special Education* 15: 281–87.

Staub, D. I., S. Schwartz, C. Galluci, and C. Peck. 1994. "Four Portraits of Friendship at an Inclusive School." *Journal of the Association for Persons with Severe Handicaps* 19: 314–25.

Thousand, J. S., R. A. Villa, and A. I. Nevin. 1994. *Creativity and Collaborative Learning: A Practical Guide for Empowering Students and Teachers*. Baltimore: Brookes.

Turnbull, A., R. Turnbull, M. Shank, and D. Leal. 1999. *Exceptional Lives*. Upper Saddle River, NJ: Merrill.

Villa, R. A., J. S. Thousand, H. Meyers, and A. I. Nevin. 1996. "Teacher and Administrator Perceptions of Heterogeneous Education." *Exceptional Children* 63: 29–45.

Wagner, D. September 1991. *National Longitudinal Transition Study of Special Education Students*. A special report prepared for the Office of Special Education, U. S. Department of Education.

Two

Numbers and Letters,
Stand Still!

Up and Over

Up and Over
And in-between,
The Letters,
Words,
Paragraphs
Wash Over Me.
Like a thunderstorm
In Georgia on a summer afternoon Full
of Sound
and
Fury
I am drenched
and overwhelmed
I search the puddles
(now muddy)
I sift and sort
and wash clean the concepts.
I then send these thoughts
to You.
I struggle to be understood
by you
Do you understand?
I am now Clear as Mud.

—Carolyn Phillips

*T*here is a specific feeling I have about letters, words, and numbers. Perhaps the description that best fits my feelings would be "chaotic emptiness." The chaotic part is that the symbols swirl around in my head, never sticking in one place long enough for my mind to lock onto them; the emptiness part is that they have no meaning or soul. For years I was fascinated about why my mother would stay up late at night and read, not to mention her ability to get lost within her books. It seemed to me that everywhere I turned, people were entranced with the written word—a government conspiracy, I was sure. The bus stations, airports, supermarkets, libraries, streets . . . everywhere I looked was the written word. It just didn't make sense to me why—or better yet, how—anyone could fall in love with written language. I hated it! It invaded my life in every area and caused me to develop an intense dislike of school from the beginning. My strongest feelings of chaotic emptiness are attached to years of homework rituals.

I rub my eyes as I flip open my fifth grade social studies book. I hate this book! It looks and feels like a tree sandwich, sliced thick on the outside and extra thin on the inside. I have many times felt sorry for the trees that were sacrificed for all the social studies books that have been wasted on me, always shadowing me. I can't seem to lose this sandwich. It's in my locker, on my back, at my desk . . . and here at the dining room table. What a terrible thing to do to a tree! Trees are meant for climbing to the sky, building forts, carving initials, swinging through the air, and, most importantly, hiding from parents. I guess I don't get it. Why would anyone want to slice and dice a perfectly good tree for a book? I'm sure this is the same book that I had last year, and even the year before. It's got to be a trick—a con game. The pile of letters inside the cover has not changed. The only difference year after year is the shiny new cover that displays the "picture of the year," a picture that lets me know that this book is a social studies book rather than one of its counterparts—history, math, English—or one of those other heavy sandwiches that follow me year after year.

A familiar presence enters the room, hovering, speaking not a word. Our eyes meet . . . a nightly ritual: mom and son, battling it out over homework. However my mom and I have an understanding. By this time in my school career, we have fought every fight and tested each other's limits; she has become a master at finding my hiding places, even the ones in the trees. I glance at the top of the page. Placing my palm on the page, I rub it hard. Up and down, up and down. I imagine how cool it would be to be able to read with the palm of my hand . . . to have all of those menacing letters absorb into my bloodstream to be carried to my brain for dissection and understanding. If only this were a real possibility rather than a fantasy. Instead, I must use my eyeballs to read this text. I must have the weakest eyeballs on this planet! They tire easily and leave me stranded, most often at the beginning of the page. My eyeballs are unlike my legs. You see, I'm the fastest guy in the fifth grade. I can run and run without ever getting tired. I am a champion runner, but a loser when it comes to reading. My legs understand what needs to be done in order to win a race. But my eyeballs get lost trying to perceive the random shotgun blast of letters, numbers, and symbols that come at me off the page.

Closing my eyes to rest, I reopen them to search for the one thing in books that makes sense to me: pictures. Where are they? This page has none. What will I do? Pictures are my guides, leading me through a fantasy world that the letters and words lock me out of. Taking a moment, I flip through the next few pages, hoping to suck out the meaning of this chapter. Pictures of Indians and Pilgrims are scattered across the pages. I look closely at them all, assessing each one, hoping that they will show me the story that is apparently spelled out in ink. But it's another lost cause, another race my eyeballs will lose.

Intuitively, Mom sits down beside me. Without any questions, she begins to read aloud to me, somehow able to make sense of all those ink blobs in front of us. Nine-thirty comes. As I crawl into bed, I take a deep breath and fall into my own pity pit, which is close to overflowing. I am stupid, stupid, stupid! Staring out my window, I lock my eyes on the moon, wishing that my teachers could make those letters and numbers stand still. If they were really good teachers, they would be able to fix my brain.

As an adult thinking back to the time in my life when I was a little kid struggling to understand why I could not read, I realize how naïve my beliefs were about myself as well as about my teachers. I was a ten-year-old boy blaming myself and my teachers for my lack of ability to recognize words and comprehend their meaning. I needed the letters and words to stand still on the page. The letters held no meaning for me because I could not attach sounds to most of them. The words undulated on the page like amoebae. Sentences represented a marathon during which I had to constantly stop and start at each individual letter, getting more confused and anxious the farther I read.

I don't remember ever being officially labeled as an "anxious" child. You know, the type of child who tapped his pencil constantly on the desk or broke into hives when a stranger would enter the room. However, as I have grown older I have reexamined the amount of stress and anxiety that I was dealing with as a child growing up with a hidden disability. Everyone has experienced anxiety-causing situations. As a student athlete, I was always under pressure to beat the guy next to me or to make a specific cut-off time. This pressure at times caused me to be anxious. However, in looking back to my childhood, I now know that same feeling I felt on the starting block was with me every day in the classroom. My controlled anxiety was deep within me and never left. It ran as an undercurrent all the time. It traveled with me wherever I went. I obviously had control of my anxiety, but what I realize now is that it fed off me for years without my dealing with it. Reading was one of the major players in my anxiety. Like plaque eating away at teeth and gums, anxiety slowly ate away at what little self-confidence I had at the time. Even though my anxiety did not show on the outside, it would flare up when I was presented with any sort of reading material: books, menus, cards, tests, signs, magazines, comic books, or whatever. The anxiety came from a feeling of failure for not being able to read or comprehend what was placed before me. As my eyes would scan the secret code, letter by letter, I would strain to decipher things. Depending on the day and my state of mind, my reading ability would fluctuate. In fact, it was a mystery to my teachers why I was able to read relatively well one day and not at all the next. I felt that I read better when I was in a good state of mind. This would happen on a few occasions when the forces of the planets were properly aligned, my friends weren't teasing me, my mom wasn't mad with me and I had placed well in a swimming competition. On those days, I was able to figure out (decode) more words than usual, which led to comprehending my reading material a little better.

Decoding

A learning disability that specifically affects reading and spelling is often referred to as *dyslexia*, a term with which I am all too familiar. Teachers cannot help me or other students with dyslexia break the reading code by using the same techniques they use with other students because we don't perceive the same code as everyone else. Phonics rules and word-attack skills are based on the premise that sounds consistently go with certain letters and that letters are placed in words in certain patterns. I perceive letters, words, and symbols differently than everyone else. My brain is a factory that produces its own secret codes. This factory in my head processes the written word in a chaotic fashion, working in a manner that does not correspond to other student factories. At times I feel that the employees running my factory are from a variety of different countries, each trying to help me perceive the written word in his or her own language.

I have spent many hours trying to understand my reading process. I know that the first stumbling block I encounter is my lack of ability to connect sounds and symbols. This is not caused by poor auditory or visual acuity; my eyesight is fine and my hearing is strong. However, somewhere in my brain I am not able to make the link between certain letters and their sounds. For instance, I confuse four out of the five vowels, meaning that when I see an O, I might say the sound for I or E. Quite often when I see a U, I say the sound for O. The sounds and symbols for E, I, O, and U are interchangeable in my mind. They always have been and probably always will be. At any point in time, my brain may confuse letter sounds and symbols; however, one letter I can always count on misperceiving is R, which my brain does not seem to process at all. This is evident in my speech; any word with an "r" comes out somewhat distorted so that a boy from the South often sounds as if he has a Northern drawl.

The more letters are put together, the more difficult they are to read. People have tried to teach me the rules of phonics, along with vowels and blends and digraphs, and I can be successful at times in applying those rules and reproducing sound combinations. However, when I try to apply what I have learned to attack a word, I am usually unsuccessful, because the individual vowel sounds and combinations change their sounds and forms when they all get together, in most cases making it a guessing game. It's like a crowded party where all the sounds and faces run together. For example, the word *church* should be easy to sound out according to the sounds and rules of phonics. However, the middle two letters—*ur*—elude me because of my brain's inability to maintain the connection between the U and its sound, the R and its sound, and the entirely new sound created by the U and R together. It's much like walking along the shore and looking back to discover that your footprints are vanishing before your eyes. The part of my brain that recognizes groups of letters or words decodes the letters much like the game, "Musical Chairs." The letters seem to fall into the chairs in a different order every time I look at them. For example, it is often difficult for me to recognize my own name. Sometimes the *s* and the *i* switch places, so that my name comes out as *Chrsitopher.* At other times when I read my name, certain letters are missing, especially ones in the middle, so that my name might read as *Chrtopher* or *Christher* or *Chrtpher.* Christmas is a terribly confusing time of year for me because the word *Christmas* is so similar to *Christopher.* When I was younger, I found it almost impossible to distinguish between the two. Looking around and seeing my name everywhere, I knew Christmas had to be a very special holiday.

The second part of reading, after one learns to decode the sounds and symbols, is attaching meaning to those words, or comprehension. As one might imagine, it is difficult to comprehend the meaning of words when you can't decode the words themselves. I have been told that one of the keys to comprehension is the ability to predict what is going to happen. Teachers ask questions to help students figure out what they are about to read. The ability to predict appears to be one of my strengths. If I can decode just a few words in a sentence, I can make an educated prediction about what the sentence means. Then I can add the key words from all the sentences together with my intuition and prediction skills to make a pretty good guess about the meaning of a paragraph.

If I could go back and talk to my teachers, I would tell them that making me read aloud did not help my reading ability at all. Having me read aloud focused only on my decoding abilities, which were essentially nonexistent. When allowed to read silently, I developed my own survival skills. In fifth grade, I was a gambler in training. I gambled on the combination of a few key words to give meaning to an entire paragraph, and I counted on luck to help me know when to answer questions in class or keep quiet. I was able to gather some important facts, which I use every day of my life; however, there are big chunks of information that are missing. I know this now because when I go to retrieve information I was supposed to have learned—from history, science, math, and so on—the information is not there. Key words sometimes float to the surface; however, I never seem to be able to recall "the big picture."

Using the Table of Contents at the beginning of a book is a way to get "the big picture," and I regularly use that strategy now. However, when I was in school, I never understood the true intention of what the Table of Contents was supposed to do. I made no linkage from the Table of Contents to the rest of the book. To take this a step further, I also didn't understand why the chapters were in the order they were. Every book was a maze of words. I never saw a beginning or ending or understood where I was going in the big scheme of things. It would have been nice to have had an aerial view of the maze I was in. Then the path would have been clearer. Teachers should not assume that what is obvious to them and most other students is obvious to the student with learning disabilities. I did not truly get the importance of the Table of Contents until it was described to me as a kitchen table with dinner courses laid out in a sequential manner. As a child, I must have taken the word *table* literally, not understanding the difference between a table of items and a table at which you eat. I believe I got confused at an early age about why the word *table* was being used in this context. Because I did not understand the difference, I rarely used the Table of Contents in any setting. I now understand that there is a certain order in which the information needs to be presented to me. I understand this because I can visualize the content as the different entrees on a table. Chapter One is the appetizer. Chapter Two is the salad. This is only one example of many concepts I have misunderstood through the years. To this day, I have great difficulty recognizing that words can look the same and sound the same but have two completely different meanings.

I wish my teachers could have spent a day in my head. Teachers have such a love of books that I think they might overuse the written word as a teaching tool. I have trouble remembering any teacher who deviated from the textbook when teaching. I was *afraid* of that book. I needed to be introduced to that book. We needed to shake hands. One of the largest mistakes most of my teachers made was to *assume* that I was on the same page in the book as everyone else. I am not talking about the actual page number, but "place," in the sense that I was going into the lesson with the same knowledge base as everyone else in the class. It would have been helpful if my teachers had started their lessons in a manner so creative that it would have intrigued all the students, while at the same time establishing a foundation for students like me. For example, in dealing with history, instead of a teacher having students start by opening the history book to a certain page to begin a lesson, it would have been helpful for my teachers to introduce the chapter in a creative manner that reviewed the time period and laid the foundation for what was to come. One of the most effective ways I got information into my brain with any given subject was to have a good introduction to the material before jumping into it. Just as a runner needs to warm up before starting a run, a student with learning disabilities also needs a warm-up time to prepare for the journey ahead. When developing individual lesson plans, I think it would be helpful for teachers to begin with an "attention-getter" that is designed to draw students' attention to the lesson, to establish the relevance of the lesson to their lives, and to lay the foundation for the information to come.

It wasn't until my public speech class in college that I understood the important contributions that Dr. Martin Luther King made to our history. The class was studying his famous "I Have a Dream" speech. I realized quickly that my classmates had much more of a foundation on this important figure than I did. I felt alone in the class. I was frustrated with why I did not know more about Dr. King. How did I miss this important lesson, which I now know is a vital part of history and is addressed throughout the education curriculum? My college professor, as most teachers would, assumed that all of us in the class were "on the same page." He had no idea that after class, I had to go back and fill in the holes in my Swiss cheese brain before I could start the class assignment. While everyone else was able to immediately begin to analyze the speech, I had to go back and figure out who Martin Luther King was. It amazes me, and saddens me for personal reasons, as to why I got so little out of my academic years while my friends and colleagues were enriched with so much. Sometimes I long to have those years back, and I find myself in the evening staring at the moon wishing that my brain was not made of Swiss cheese.

Comprehension

I wish my teachers had focused on helping me with comprehension instead of decoding. I always felt like I never got past first base in reading. There I stood, watching the game go on around me. Year after year, the books would fly by me. I would see these books as they slid past first base, but I was never able to grab on to them and follow them around the bases. At first base, I could hold the book and look at the pictures and guess what the book was about. At second base, it was my responsibility to make sense of (decode) the squiggles on the pages and try to turn them into words. If I accomplished that successfully, I could then go to third base, where I would get an understanding of what I was reading. The goal of any baseball player (reader) is to make it all the way around the bases to reach home plate—to "own" the book.

I could never get past first base. Because of the way my brain processes information, I could not make sense of the squiggles. This put a barrier between me and third base. I now know that I can get to Base Three, where comprehension takes place, without ever having to touch Base Two. I can take a short cut. If I can run from Base One to Base Three, I have a second chance of catching the book before it passes me by. My goal in the Game of Reading is to *comprehend* what is in front of me, no matter what method I have to use.

For years, my teachers worked hard on teaching me how to decode. I learned from them that reading was figuring out the words. It wasn't until my English 102 class during my sophomore year in college that I reached third base and started to understand what reading was all about. The teacher's name was Amelia Davis-Horne, and she was effective because she made the words come alive. She gave life to the pages in front of me. In that class, it didn't matter that the words did not stand still. What mattered was that, for the first time, the words made sense. Although there were pages of reading requirements, the class was never about reading; it was about meaning—transporting ourselves from the classroom right into the story.

That English 102 class was the start of the development of my own comprehension action plan. Ms. Davis-Horne taught me the basics. She made first base a great place to be. Her introductions to the stories brought instant interest, even to subjects that had previously held little interest for me. The story could be about bird watching—when I was nineteen, I could not imagine anything more boring—and she would be able to make it interesting. This teacher would be able to transport me into the mind of a bird watcher. She did this by setting the stage. She used whatever props she needed in order to entice us. If that meant bringing in a bird, she brought in a bird. She was a master at developing scenery. Her podium became a stage that would change story by story. She used videos when we were to read anything about historic events. Intertwined throughout the stories, she would often play music. The music was never really connected to the plot of the stories but was used to create a mood. If it was a sad story, we might hear some mournful music from Chopin, while Beethoven played for us to drive home a powerful point. Role playing was another one of her favorite teaching strategies. She turned students into actors who would become characters in a scene. Even the most complex material would come clear to me. For the first time, I was able to talk intelligently about these stories. Because she immersed my mind totally in the story, I wanted to get involved—which is the key to teaching children to read.

If teachers focus on comprehension, students are going to *want* to read. To develop my own reading comprehension action plan, I have analyzed what helps me comprehend best. I have also traveled across the country and listened to children who are like me. There are basic things that I hear that work for other students struggling to understand the written word, and from those children as well as from adults like me who still struggle to read, I would like to pass along the following suggestions to teachers.

Don't Assume the Obvious

Children are always asking questions: What are we having for dinner? When are we going to Six Flags? How many days till Christmas? Having answers to these questions is essential for children to organize their day-to-day lives and helps them to anticipate and prepare for what is to come. Children naturally want to know what to expect. Use this same philosophy to start off every lesson. For instance, start by going to the Table of Contents and training your students to do this. This will help orient the students to where they are in the book, remind them of what they have already studied, and show them where they are going. Most students with learning disabilities have the ability to understand the structure of their day. They should be able to comprehend the gist of what they are studying, even if they can't comprehend the words in every passage. Don't assume that what is obvious to you and most other students is also obvious to the student with learning disabilities. The Table of Contents is, in fact, made up of words!

Alive and Kicking: Make New Vocabulary Words Come Alive

Always introduce new vocabulary words in an interesting manner, and then directly link them to where they are placed in the book. It is important to remember that *you* are responsible for making the words come alive. Don't assume that your students will automatically recognize the word when they meet it in the passage. Help them out by giving them colored transparent tape to lay over the new words in their books or some other medium that will help pull out the words from the passage. This will help make the connection and give life to the passage.

Picture Reading

It would have been helpful for me to have a visual outline of the stories and books that teachers wanted me to read as a child. One of the most effective ways for me to comprehend "the big picture" of anything I read is to use a graphic organizer. Although I have difficulty decoding symbols, my brain recognizes visual diagrams and pictures with ease. These pictures are processed as a unified whole, a complete thought, whereas letters, words, and numbers are fragmented into puzzle pieces in my brain. For example, when I see a picture of a cake, it stays with me. I recognize it immediately and attach meaning to it. When I see the word *cake*—c/a/k/e—I often fail to recognize it, because the letters are like pieces of a recipe that have been torn apart and thrown at me. They offer little meaning, and they are clouded with negative feelings. Graphic organizers use pictures and diagrams to illustrate concepts and organize text into a sequence that is easy for me to store and retrieve.

I started using graphic organizers when I was in college, although I had no idea that was what they were called. I was allowed to substitute a series of selected courses in place of my foreign language requirements. Ironically, the selected courses were all literature courses offered by the English department. (A lot of good that did! The printed word, even written in English, is, at times, foreign to me.) Having taken a total of six literature courses, it was as if I had minored in a foreign language. However, it was through these courses that I perfected my use of graphic organizers to comprehend large amounts of complex reading material. In one year, I had to read the *Iliad*, the *Odyssey*, Virgil's *Aenead*, and Dante's *The Inferno*. It was the first time I had truly "tasted" literature and was exposed to the feeling of what knowledge was all about. I finally understood why my mother stayed up night after night reading book after book. Through these adventures, a new world opened. Even though I rarely spoke in class discussions of these assignments, my mind was bursting with activity. I started visualizing myself on the journeys taken by the heroes of these stories. With Rosemary Jackson, I developed my own reading style. At first nothing would stick, whether I had Rosemary read the stories aloud to me or whether I was listening to them on tape or attempting to read them myself. It took another step to achieve comprehension and retention. It all started with a doodle that Rosemary drew in an effort to explain a piece of the story to me. However, it ended with the pencil in my hand, diagramming the story in pictures as she read to me. One of my better doodles was Odysseus's confrontation with the Cyclops, which I'm sure haunted Rosemary's nightmares that evening. I spared no red ink on the gory details and passed the discussion test a few weeks later with red ink in hand. The graphic organizer was a perfect fit for me. It allowed me a way of getting the information out of the book and into my mind.

I think there are two types of students who might use graphic organizers for reading. Some students will pick up the technique naturally, while other students may need to be taken through the steps of how to use this technique effectively. Teachers can use graphic organizers with the entire class by diagramming the reading material with words and pictures while simultaneously talking through the process.

There are books available with preconceived graphic organizers especially designed for specific types of reading material, such as biographies, sequential events, comparison and contrast, and so forth. There is also software available that allows you to create your own computer-generated organizer. For some students, this process comes naturally, and the best thing is to give these students a pad of paper and turn them loose to create their own organizers. Some helpful tips for using graphic organizers to help improve reading comprehension in students with learning disabilities include the following:

• Show examples of the various looks an organizer can have so students will understand that there is no "right" or "wrong" way to complete them.
• Make sure your students are on the right track as they progress through the reading material. Don't allow them to complete the organizer incorrectly; communicate with them throughout the process.

- Let your students be natural with the designs they come up with: boxes, circles, pictures—they should be encouraged to use whatever works.
- Be particularly careful with timelines and other sequenced information; check often to be sure that students correctly sequence a series of events. It should not matter whether the sequence goes from top to bottom, bottom to top, right to left, left to right, or even diagonally across the page as long as the events are placed in the correct sequence from the starting point.
- Have students try out different mediums for creating their graphic organizers, such as lined paper, blank paper, colored paper, manipulative objects, colored pencils, crayons, markers, computers, and so on. Often, the farther away one gets from traditional paper and pencil, the more memorable and meaningful the final product will be.

Primal Teaching:
Tap into Your Students' Emotions

One reading comprehension strategy that has always worked for me is my teachers' abilities to tap into my emotions. This strategy is easier said than done. As a student, I always carried around deep frustration, anxiety, and anger. The most effective teachers were the ones who were able to use my emotions to tie me into the context of whatever we were reading. There are several core characteristics that many students with learning disabilities share: a basic lack of self-worth, the feeling that everyone is watching you, and a feeling that you're going to get caught at "faking it." Teachers can draw on these emotions to make their students feel passionate about reading. Books that I remember from my high school years are books that made an emotional impact on me. For some reason, my connection with the book overrode my disability. A good example of this is from high school, when I sat through the class-reading of a difficult book: *A Tale of Two Cities*. I was able to relate personally to the characters in the book, particularly Madam DeFarge. At that time in my life, I was very angry and really involved in manipulating myself through the education system. I identified with the character of Madam DeFarge because she was strong and was not going to let anyone beat her. I know that my English teacher at that time had no idea that she had tapped into a unique strategy that worked for me, but, to this day, the few books I do remember are the ones that I am in some way emotionally connected to. Most of my areas of difficulty are tied to the part of my brain that's in charge of language; therefore, comprehension strategies that work the best come when that part of my brain is bypassed and the most primal part, the emotional part, is stimulated.

Books on Tape: Have Students Listen to Good Reading

Students with dyslexia have difficulty decoding symbols, in part, because the symbols don't "stick" to the page. One of the most effective reading strategies I have ever used is one that combines visual and auditory input. Books on tape have given me a new perspective on life. Through the use of this medium I have been able to go places that I was not capable of going before. It started as a survival skill. Due to the large amount of required reading I had in college, I was unable to keep up with the work. Something had to be done, so we began to order my textbooks on tape. For the first time that I could remember, I actually began to keep up with and understand my reading assignments. From talking with teachers and students, I am aware that people know about books on tape but typically view them as an accommodation rather than a reading-improvement strategy, and thus, de-emphasize the use of taped texts. This assumption is a mistake. I strongly believe that books on tape should be implemented on a daily basis with students who have difficulty with reading for three major reasons: (1) The combination of audio and visual cues combines two modalities for better comprehension, (2) following the text while listening helps your eyes learn to track the words more smoothly, and (3) the process builds better word recognition.

Multisensory learning is one of the best techniques for working with students who have processing deficits. Using books on tape while following along in a text involves both sight and hearing. I often follow the line of words with my finger or a ruler, adding a third modality. Hearing, seeing, and touching the words at the same time immediately heightens the clarity. I can almost feel the different parts of my brain being stimulated. I began using books on tape with a clunky, bright yellow, four-track tape recorder especially designed for people who are blind or visually impaired, but I have now upgraded to a sporty Walkman model. This allows me to add a fourth modality—movement, which is how I've always learned best. By reading, listening, feeling, and moving, my brain decodes the words much more efficiently, which increases my comprehension tremendously.

To my surprise, another benefit that arose from using books on tape was the development of the muscles in my eyes. No longer do I read with the same stopping and starting motion that plagued me for years. From years of hearing and following smooth reading, my eyes now transition smoothly from letter to letter and word to word.

Finally, I now recognize more words when reading on my own. It is hard for me to quantify the number of words I now recognize compared to those I knew before I started using books on tape; however, my confidence about smaller words, such as *there, was, has,* and so forth, has increased. Seeing, hearing, and touching the words over and over has improved my ability to decode on my own.

I now use books on tape throughout every part of my life, whether in school, in work, or in the social realm. Without this tool, it would be very difficult for me to access the information from magazines and books that is available to everyone around me. I wish that books on tape had been available to me as a child. As an adult, it is an invaluable tool.

Colored Transparencies

Another mechanism that I have found very effective for myself and others who have difficulty decoding letters, symbols, and words is the use of colored transparency sheets. The easiest way for me to explain why this technique works is that it helps pull the reading material out from the page, giving it a type of three-dimensional effect. The scientific explanation is that colors can sometimes slow the letters and words from reaching the brain just enough to give the dyslexic brain a little more time to process the information. I have found it very helpful to use colored transparency overlays when I am reading a book or any other document from which I need to draw important details. I have experimented with several types of colors and have found that blue, gray, yellow, and green are the most effective for me. I have found that the red is ineffective, and, in fact, tends to make decoding more difficult. When I use this technique, it really does feel like the information I am trying to decode is slowed down by the colors, allowing my brain to process the information more efficiently. Cutting the transparency sheet into a small rectangular marker and placing it on the page to use as a guide is also helpful. I have seen some students tape the strips onto hand-made cardboard rulers so that when the ruler is placed over the sentence to be read, the transparency highlights the words.

Colored transparencies do not work for everyone, and, depending on the reading disability, may or may not be effective. I would suggest trying several colors before choosing one. There are two good sources of transparencies. Office or school supply stores will usually carry the page-length transparency sheets. A second source is your local high school or community theater, which uses transparency strips, called gel paper, for stage lighting. In fact, drama departments will sometimes have sample books from which they order. These sample books contain over two hundred colors of ready-made strips that make wonderful markers.

Magnifying Aids

Even though I have good eyesight, an effective way for my brain to get information from a page of squiggles is by using magnifying aids. There are several types of magnifying aids on the market. Most are developed for senior citizens or people with visual impairments. One of the most effective is the magnifying page, which is like a sheet of paper that is transparent to the eye and has the effect of a magnifying glass. Placing the magnifying sheet over a paragraph helps enlarge the print and makes it easier to read the text. If this strategy is helpful, there are other magnifying devices that use light and distance to help the reader. It is important to remember that learning disabilities are perceptual disabilities and not connected to physical problems with the eyes; however, some aides designed for individuals with visual impairments can be helpful in aiding the brain to perceive. Of course, enlarging print is a popular accommodation; however, a low-cost magnifying sheet is portable, unobtrusive, and available to almost any reading situation. To locate these magnifying aides, contact an independent-living vendor for a catalog (see the Appendix).

Highlighters and Highlighting Tape

I use highlighters to help me decipher words that look similar and need emphasis. For instance, due to the way my brain processes symbols, I cannot distinguish between similar words. When reading a passage, I have trouble distinguishing between *has* and *was, been* and *done, there* and *they,* and numerous other pairs of words. Numbers are just as difficult. Nines and sixes, threes and eights, and twos and fives consistently elude me. Using colored highlighters or colored highlighter tape, I mark the similar words in different colors so that I know they are different words when I reach them. I use this strategy when I am reading something important, in which the details have to be clear.

In addition to highlighting similar words, I have at times made myself a definition chart to use while reading. For instance, when I took biology in college, many of the words started with the prefix *phy-* and looked similar. I had difficulty with not only decoding the words, but also remembering their meanings. Rosemary would often write the words and definitions at the top of the page and then select colors to highlight each one so that when I encountered that word in the passage, I could refer to the chart. Eventually, I would connect the color to the word and definition and use the chart less and less.

Although this is a great study technique, the public schools usually frown upon letting students highlight books or write in their margins. Students with learning disabilities may need to purchase their textbooks so they can use the strategies they need to use; however, the recent invention of highlighter tape is a removable alternative to permanent highlighter pens. Students can use the tape as study aids just as they would use highlighter pens. The tape is also handy for teachers who may want to preview chapters and highlight the important information before students take them home to read. This helps students learn how to use highlighters to pull out only the most important information.

Conclusion

If I had only known as a child what I now know about reading, my life would have been a little easier. As an adult with a reading disability, I have learned how to use effective strategies and technology that I have discovered on my own. I now know the joy of literature. Whether I read a book or listen to it on tape, my life is enriched by the written word. I've also learned that there is no magic pill to correct my reading disability. It follows me around, never leaving my side, whether I am faced with reading a menu, a birthday card, or a road sign. To be effective, strategies must be able to follow me through these different environments. The most effective strategies are the ones that are portable and nonintrusive. It is my experience that when these strategies become a habit in my day-to-day life, I read more effectively and efficiently. Reading becomes a habit rather than a struggle. I have made reading a part of my life. Just as I get up every morning to go to work, I also read the newspaper on the Internet with my screen reader.

The philosophy in most school systems is that children are failures if they cannot read on their expected grade levels. When this happens, teachers, parents, and students panic. At that point, they frequently pull back to what has worked for everyone else instead of thinking "outside the box" and experimenting with things that *might* work for that individual student. I have my own individualized reading plan. I know how I read best: I like to read standing up, not sitting down; the lights cannot be too bright or dim; absolutely no fluorescent lights are allowed; I use color whenever I can—black and white bores me; if the environment is too noisy, I use earplugs; if it's too quiet, I make my own noise; sometimes I walk backwards when I read—for some reason, this relieves anxiety; I read best in the morning and worst at night; I always ask for help when I can—life is too short to be stuck on a word; my favorite strategy is to have someone read for me. About 30 percent of the time, I read off a computer, using screen-reading software; about 20 percent of the time, I listen to tapes; and the additional 50 percent of my reading is on my own, using a variety of self-selected strategies. This last 50 percent is the hardest and is not by choice.

As a child, I lay in bed and cried because I could not read like everyone else. As an adult, I no longer cry for myself but for all the other children who may never learn to love the written word as I have. To them, their books will always be tree sandwiches, and their hiding places will be harder to find.

So, I urge the teachers and parents who are reading this book not to let your children go to bed staring sadly at the moon because they can't make the words stand still, when the important thing is to make the words come alive.

Three

The Dyslexic Writer

Catcher in the Rye
Ouuchhaa!
That hurt.

Monday, 8:00 a.m.,
I gave you my ideas
in the form of a paper
My ideas had taken form
And had their own life.
I, so excited to share
these concepts with you,
did not sleep for two days.

Friday. 8:40 a.m.,
You gave me your ideas,
And my paper was now
washed in red . . . bleeding.
Circled and slashed—beyond
repair . . . no idea I have
could survive your attention
to details . . . details that don't
matter. I completed your job
by shredding and trashing that
paper . . . I have not slept well
Since.
                                  —Carolyn Phillips

Gloria

A bird, eagerly looks to find her way into an opening in the church window. Wings beating, she watches from the small window ledge at the roof line. I watch her, like many others sitting in the pews, as my grandmother Gloria's eulogy is being read by her youngest son, Joe, my uncle. Aware of Nana's presence, I let out a deep sigh as the tears come. She is here in all her glory, giving us one more chance to feel her love. As I watch the bird rest at the window, I listen to Uncle Joe review Nana's life through humor, pain, and love that can only be seen through the eyes of the youngest child. I find myself amazed at the wonder of my grandmother Nana's time on this earth. With her casket lying in front of me, for the first time I truly feel the power of her life. Six kids and alone at age thirty-five in the 1940s, Gloria put her faith in God and worked hard to make a life for her children. Alone and poor, she didn't give up, a testimony to her character. Joe reads with a hollow and lost voice as tears travel down his checks searching for a resting place. "I will miss my mother dearly."

At the end of the Mass, I, along with other cousins and nephews, walk the casket out of the church. I feel different but not sad. A sensation of honor and strength comes over me as I hold my grandmother above the earth.

At the gravesite the tears do not stop as each family member takes time to touch Nana's coffin and cry words of love in her honor—a time of closure, I think. As I embrace my five-year-old niece, Emily, I watch my mother walk up and place her palm on the casket, with a rose held up to her lips. I listen to her as she speaks to Nana. Glancing up to the sky, I feel the tears come forth hard again, but this time they are joined by the feelings of honor and strength I had felt earlier. My love for my family consumes me. How could I have missed it before? I see life so much clearer now. At this moment, I know what life is all about. *Love*, pure and simple, my heart aches with this new-found truth. What a great gift for Nana to give us. Glancing at Emily, I watch her eyes, hoping that she is old enough to catch this gift.

At the end of the services, I stay with my cousin, Abe, and nephew, Stuart, to make sure Nana is put to rest in the ground.

The place is warm; green grass hugs and blankets the ground. A fresh scent of salt from the Gulf of Mexico penetrates the air. Gloria will like it here. There is a large tree that hangs over her resting place, offering shade and protection. What a perfect place for a bird, I think. She will be happy here. We love you Gloria.

———————

There are critical turning points in one's life that spark such high emotional feelings that it is impossible to keep them inside. The recent death of my grandmother was one of those times, and it felt natural for me to want to express my thoughts and feelings in writing. Turning points such as this stay with us for a lifetime and are carried into our everyday lives. One of my most memorable turning points was the time I tried and tried to pass my drivers license test—the symbol of transition from childhood to adulthood in the minds of many teenagers. This turning point will always stay with me. The struggle of trying to obtain a plastic card into adulthood resulted in such feelings of defeat that I thought I would never recover. Another turning point in my life was the time I got accepted to the University of Georgia, and, more importantly, became a member of the university swim team. Holding the letter of acceptance in my hand, I could not imagine anything more fulfilling in my life. As I look back on these two incidents, I realize the power of emotional gratification and destruction: the emotional energy that comes from inside when life offers a glimpse into destiny. Nana Gloria was destined to die, as are we all, and the love and loss that I felt during her funeral will always stay with me and be forged as one of the most important turning points in my life. We all handle defeat and success in our own individual manners, choosing various outlets to express the remarkable energy that comes from life. Over the last few years, my outlet of choice has been writing, which has become a vital part of my emotional balance, allowing me a gratifying outlet for my thoughts and feelings. I have learned to use writing as a way of reflecting back on major transitions in my life.

Not only is writing an emotional outlet for me, but it has become a way of learning through organization and discipline. Writing takes two directions for me. The first direction is one of written expression—putting my thoughts on paper in a way to satisfy not only my emotional feelings, but also my desire for creativity. The second direction has been an unexpected bonus. Writing has become a vehicle for my right brain to talk to my left brain. I am a right-brained (visual, creative) learner, possibly because most of my disability lies in my left brain. Through practice and discipline, I have developed a comfortable, relaxed writing style that allows me to have access to my left brain by "coming in the back door."

In order for me to utilize writing as an emotional and creative outlet, I first had to develop a respect for literature. Growing up as a dyslexic learner, this was a challenge for both me and my teachers. Their goal was always to focus on basic remediation, which, in the scheme of things, makes sense. If you have a car that has a blow-out, the first thing you would do is fix it by changing the tire or plugging it. The goal is to get the car back on the road so you can get to your desired destination. My teachers focused on fixing me and getting me to the next grade. What we now know about dyslexia is that you can't "fix" it.

Teachers are now more prepared to work with students whose brains process information differently. There is now more of a focus on modifications, which, with the use of technology, have opened new doors of expression for the dyslexic writer. The dyslexic writer can now place his or her thoughts on paper by using appropriate adaptive software and hardware, de-emphasizing the logistics of writing and emphasizing the expression of creative thoughts. This evolution is much like the evolution of our society that was brought about by the computer. Before the computer, we had file cabinets and more file cabinets full of written documents cluttering and overwhelming our offices. With the more accessible use of the computer, information can be stored in a more condensed and accessible fashion, which frees up more breathing room for all of us (except in

Rosemary's office, because she refuses to give up her filing cabinets). It wasn't until I was able to de-emphasize spelling and grammar through technology that I was able to appreciate the beauty of writing. This process started out through reading and learning to understand poetry and other types of literature. Through class discussion, writing came alive, and spelling died.

Another key component of success for the dyslexic writer is practice, practice, practice. In many instances, teachers force practice through traditional methods, such as writing about specific topics or keeping daily journals. For the dyslexic writer, this forces discipline but, in some cases, creates hurdles. One thing of which I am aware about my writing method is that it is not the amount I practice so much as *how* I practice that makes a difference. Sitting at the dining room table writing on an assigned topic or in bed writing in my journal was not the most effective way for me to develop writing skills. The development of my writing method came from my one-on-one working relationship with Rosemary. Through a collaborative process, we were able to examine my cognitive processing deficits and the specific impact they have on my ability to put my thoughts down on paper. Pushing through years of my negative experiences with writing and the ineffective writing skills I had developed, we perfected a method of organizing and outlining my thoughts through open discussion. These discussion times were vital to exploring questions and building an interest in the topic. This technique allowed my intellectual thought processes to develop and expand before I put anything down on paper. It gave me a road map of where I wanted to go with the paper. It wasn't until we added the dictation component, however, that it all came together. Success was found.

Dictation was the missing component I needed in order to develop my writing skills. By the end of my junior year in college, Rosemary and I had become a writing team. She helped to standardize my writing and put it into a form that would be approved by English teachers. This left me time to concentrate on the content, language, and presentation of the work. Dictation also made it possible for me to draw on a strength. Instead of sitting at a desk forcing the language to come out on paper, I was able to stand up and pace around the room as I was dictating. The pacing helped with not only the flow of my writing, but also the development of my thought processes.

The prewriting outline development went through several phases. In the beginning, the outlines were more detailed, much like traditional outlines. As I became a stronger writer and more practiced at using outlines and dictation, I weaned myself from the more traditional outline to one that suited my own style better—one that is like the commonly used graphic organizers of today. It would have been so helpful to have been introduced to graphic organizers earlier in my academic career! There are now a variety of outlining software programs that can be beneficial to creative learners, because they allow the student to organize information in more creative, visual formats.

Once Rosemary and I were able to develop a relaxed writing style through discussion, outlining, and dictation, I began to notice that I was able to retain and recall specific language details that had, in the past, been very difficult to access. Through the collaborative writing process, I discovered that I could recall details about the title, author, and characters of books—information I had never been able remember before. In the past, these language details—names, places, and so forth—had all remained lost in the left side of my brain. Using kinesthetics and graphic organizers while writing about the books opened up new doors in my brain that had been closed all my life. This unexpected bonus of right-brain/left-brain communication added a unique learning method to my everyday life.

One aspect of writing that I have not been, and never will be, able to conquer is that of spelling. There is no beating around the bush, I just need to come out and say it—I wish spelling dead! There, I said it! Boy, that felt good—I like how this phrase roles off my tongue. It feels right. I would be in denial if I did not admit that spelling was one of my major self-esteem killers when I was growing up. I have a vision of all twenty-six letters of the alphabet scattered on the ground . . . where I have stomped on them. Spelling will always be a mystery for me. The logic behind the organization of all those symbols eludes me. I will never be a good speller, which is not easy for me to admit. I have taken the file labeled "spelling" and placed it very low on my priority list. I have learned not to allow spelling to take control of my life anymore. For too many years, the letters dictated where I had to go with my writing. I was not in a democracy; I was in a dictatorship, with the letters being the rulers. Early on, subconsciously, my brain figured out that it did not march to the same beat of all those letters. Rejection was the outcome. "F's" were the product. There is no easy way for me to explain the overwhelming conflict my brain takes on as it tries to process and dissect all those symbols.

It was my second year in college when I finally escaped from the army of letters. As my brain was exposed to the art of writing, writing came alive. The umbrella of passion protected me as I was trained not to let the rainfall of letters interfere with my imagination.

I have been asked by many teachers and parents about how much emphasis should be put on spelling in school. There is no easy answer. A lot depends on each individual's specific processing deficits. When I was going through school, an emphasis was placed on connecting sounds with symbols (phonics). Due to my auditory-processing deficit, this teaching method did not lend itself to positive results. Drawing on what I now know about my own disability, if sight recognition had been used, my visual-processing deficits would have interfered with that process also. Because my processing disabilities affect both visual and auditory processing, I really did not respond to any approach that was tried. I find it difficult to make the connections between sounds, words, sentences, and thoughts, or meaning, and when we're talking about written language, we throw in the additional element of symbol formation. Can you see why my brain starts spinning?

It may be easier for me to explain where I fit into the writing process by looking at the five dimensions of our language system. *Phonology* revolves around the sounds of our language system and the rules that define how sounds are combined to form words. If I think about this, I am aware that I have missed out on a lot of sounds since birth, due to my brain's inability to process them. This poses the question: How can I understand the rules of phonology when I process the sounds differently? I am aware that the sounds I am misperceiving occur in different parts of words. In any word with an R—beginning, middle or end—I will either misunderstand the word or fail to recognize it at all. Not only do I have difficulty perceiving the R itself, but its very presence in a word seems to throw off the other sounds. For example, I cannot tell that the words *harp* and *hop* or *woods* and *words* are different words. I have to listen to the context of the sentence in order to perceive a visual image. For years, I did this automatically, without questioning; however, now that I am older and more confident, I am more likely to ask for clarification. What I have found out through doing this is that I misperceive words much more often than I realized. Not only do my perceptual deficits affect my ability to recognize sounds, but, in turn, these misperceptions lead to my mispronouncing words without even realizing it. It is not uncommon for me to be questioned about my "accent" two to three times a day, but it is uncommon for me to be corrected or have attention drawn to the words I mispronounce. Recently, I conducted an informal research project in which I asked two friends of mine to point out words I mispronounce. I was amazed at the number of times I was corrected. It was to the point where they felt uncomfortable—and so did I.

Morphology is the part of language that deals with the structure of words and word forms. My perceptual disability affects the morphology of words in two main areas. The first area affects the construction of a simple word, as I have discussed before. My second problem area comes with the English language, which cannot seem to be satisfied to leave words in their simple forms. I can never celebrate the fact that I actually have spelled a simple word correctly, because I know someone will come along and want me to put something on the front of it (prefix) or something on the end of it (suffix) or change the middle of it for no good reason. One of the first things teachers tend to notice about my papers is that my words usually lack appropriate endings. I am now aware that I consistently leave off endings such as *ing*, *ed*, and *s*, but it took years for me to understand why my teachers would get so upset with me. I imagine that it must be similar to trying to explain the color green to someone who is color-blind. I know I don't perceive these endings when I read, so I imagine that I leave them off when writing because they don't exist in my language world. However, it could also be that I focus so hard on simply trying to spell or read or understand the main (root) word that I ignore any endings that happen to be attached. I recognize that word endings affect my pronunciation of words. For example, I have little trouble pronouncing the word *common*, but great difficulty trying to pronounce the word *commonly*. It takes someone three or four times of repeating it to me before I can correctly reproduce it. This difficulty also shows up when I'm trying to write variations of some words, such as *first* or *third*. I know this is truly perceptual, because I cannot hear the middle sounds in those words. One of my greatest areas of morphological difficulty comes when a word changes structure as it changes tenses (e.g., *come* and *came*; *see* and *saw*; *ride* and *rode*; *begin*, *began*, and *begun*). These words look the same when I read them and sound the same when I hear them, so it has been an impossible task for me to try to use them correctly when writing. Thank goodness for grammar checks and secretaries!

Syntax, the third component of language, provides rules for putting together a series of words to form sentences. Finally, we get to a word that I can not only say, but also understand without Rosemary having to explain it to me. My syntax difficulties were one of the first hurdles we worked on in our collaborative writing process. I have always been aware of a tendency to re-structure phrases when I am speaking with others. I commonly switch words around. For instance, instead of saying, "I'm going to wash my car," I might say, "I'm going to car my wash." When I am writing, I might or might not spot this mistake and correct it. A greater difficulty I have when writing is under-standing the rules of the sentence. Because I write the way I speak (and perceive), I put little emphasis on punctuation. When I am speaking, I tune in closely to the body language and facial expressions of my listener, and form the presentation of my sentences based on those nonverbal cues. I have trained my-self to be in tune with my audience when speaking, and now, when writing. This has been a very effective strategy, which I will discuss later. However, this does not help me correctly form or punctuate my sentences when writing. If left to my own devices, I would write sentences that go on and on forever and have no punctuation at all. Or, write fragments. The strategy that works for me is to think like a poet, forming sentences that are short but packed with meaning.

Semantics is a fourth aspect of language and refers to the content of what is expressed: the meaning as well as the rela-tionship between words that determines meaning. This is an area in which I rule! I am a linguist's dream—or worst night-mare. I am the king of plugging in words that don't belong. My kingdom seems fine to me, but to travelers visiting my king-dom, confusion lies ahead. In many ways, travelers can experi-ence a land similar to the one I live in every day. I often hear references from my friends to "Christopher's World," a place where they have to decipher what I say in order to get my in-tended meaning and thereby hold a logical conversation. This can prove difficult, as in the situation the other day when I was spending a weekend with friends in the mountains and started feeling under the weather. I kept referring to needing "eutha-nasia," when it was actually the herb, Echinacea, to which I was referring. No one corrected me until we got back home, which then explained the strange looks I kept getting all weekend.

I have also found myself constantly plugging in the wrong word when writing. This often happens in e-mail, where I have sometimes put myself in trouble by substituting words that have sexual connotations. This was called to my attention when I sent an e-mail to several close colleagues apologizing for not getting back in touch with them the day before because I had "screwed around with my secretary all day." What I actually meant to relate was that it had been one of those days in which I had "screwed up" everything, and I had spent the day working with my secretary, correcting things. There are several examples that have occurred while writing this book. When we are writing, Rosemary must enter Christopher's World. No matter how familiar she is with the rules of my world, I still manage to throw her a curve every now and then. In a different chapter, I wrote about the different types of charms that individuals with learning disabilities use. Rosemary typed diligently as I described the characteristics of the "Muse," a person who survives by watching others and imitating them. After an hour of working on this section, Rosemary politely suggested that we needed a different name for this charmer because the description did not match that of a muse. Being the bull-headed, stubborn type, I insisted that she was wrong and I was right. You would think that, at this time in my life, I would not question the use of a word, much less Rosemary's insight. After I defended my position by demonstrating how a muse acts, she crawled out of Christopher's World long enough to realize my intended word. She then informed me—again, politely—that I was describing a *mime*, rather than a muse. Semantics can truly offer challenges to the dyslexic writer and humor to his or her audience.

Pragmatics is the final component of language and refers to the use of communication in social contexts. When I was a senior in high school, I took an English writing course that I enjoyed. This required class caught me off guard because I thought for sure it would prevent me from graduating. However, the class ended up being a feasible challenge. The teacher designed the class around full student participation and feedback. Everyone could choose their own topics and have a week to write the paper, which would be read aloud by another student and graded by the entire class on a rubric. The rubric contained areas such as grammar, spelling, creativity, organization, and sense of audience. As scary as the idea was to have my paper read out loud in front of the class, it challenged me to write diligently all week long. My goal was to not be embarrassed in front of my classmates, so I became quickly aware of the audience for which I was writing: my peers. Pulling on my strength of nonverbal communication, I watched and listened to how the students responded as papers were read aloud in class. This gave me a feel for what the audience wanted. Based on these observations—and help from my girlfriend—my papers were not laughed at. I managed to enjoy the class and improve my writing skills. I still had yet to get the whole picture of how language is used in writing, and my stories were raw. However, because of my strong desire to relate to my audience, I gave 100 percent of myself.

From that class on, I have always understood the importance of writing with an audience in mind and have actually been quite successful in relating effectively to readers. The use of pragmatics in writing is often ignored, while it is a skill that can be fostered and taught and can ultimately become a strong component of the writing process. While other components of language will always remain difficult, my confidence in writing is boosted by knowing that I do have a strength: pragmatics.

Through examining the five parts of language from the dyslexic writer's perspective, it is easy to see how these components intertwine with each other, multiplying the possibilities for failure. Out of the five components, there is only one that felt natural to me. Yet, I have been able to train myself through practice, discipline, and the use of technology to become a successful dyslexic writer.

Tips for Teachers

Assistive Technology for Writing

It is critical to use assistive technology in the writing development process as well as for accommodations and modifications. There are now a variety of software programs and equipment available to the dyslexic writer. Without assistive technology, I would probably not have completed college and would not be able to hold my current job. Through the use of talking word processors, abbreviation/word-prediction software, a reliable word-processing spell checker, a portable spell checker, a laptop computer (portable keyboard), and voice recognition system, I am able to write at a much higher proficiency than I ever would have without these tools.

The first step in implementing assistive technology into the classroom is to make sure you feel comfortable with a computer and how the adaptive software works. In working with many teachers, I have found that there is a strong reluctance to make assistive technology a part of their classrooms. I have noted that this is due to a variety of reasons, with the most prevalent reason being lack of training. I call this phenomenon *rampant technophobia*, a term I read somewhere. The term relates to what I see when I speak to teachers. It is important that, as a teacher, if you do not feel comfortable with learning basic computer skills, you have access to someone who can provide technical assistance in the classroom. The computer has become an extension of my mind. Within the hard drive, I am able to store and retrieve information that would have been lost in a shuffle of papers. Through adaptive software, I have access to a world that I would have missed. The keyboard allows information to flow through my fingertips and into the memory of the computer.

Students cannot benefit from use of the computer until they learn the basics of keyboarding. There are many typing tutorial programs available to facilitate acquisition of keyboarding skills. The earlier students can develop keyboarding skills, the better. Check out the technology chapter for more in-depth information about keyboarding tutorial programs.

Writing Aids

There are a variety of writing aids available that offer support to students with perceptual problems in their handwriting. Some of these aids can be found locally at drug stores, while others can be purchased through independent-living catalogs.

- **Colored and Lined Paper:** Experiment with writing paper. Using paper that is different colors and/or has lines of different dimensions can be helpful in the writing process. I still remember the times when I was working on different writing assignments in elementary school. The most memorable of those times are associated with using colored paper. I actually can recall specific writing assignments through remembering the color of paper. Experiment with different types of lined paper. Graphing paper is often helpful for students who have spatial problems, particularly when learning to form letters or when doing math calculations. There is also paper for beginning writers that has raised lines to help students learn to stay between the lines. It is important to match the student with the lined paper that best suits his or her needs.
- **Pencil Grippers:** Experiment with different types of pencil grippers. You can purchase them or make your own. Some teachers push pencils and pens through tennis or foam balls to make grippers. Match the size of the gripper to the student's hand. Make sure it feels comfortable to the student and that it helps the writing. This tool encourages the student to put pressure on the gripper instead of forcing the pressure down on the paper. Many dyslexic writers are unable to write with a pencil because they constantly break off the tip. Some grippers have been developed specifically for individuals with motor skill problems and physical disabilities.
- **Writing Guides:** There are a variety of writing guides available for students who have difficulty writing on a

straight line or staying within boundaries. A majority of these guides are made of plastic or cardboard. They can be helpful in academic settings as well as in social settings. For instance, if one wants to write a message on a card, a plastic writing guide placed over the card will help the student keep the written message aligned.

- **Enlarged Writing Materials:** It may be helpful for students to utilize material that has been enlarged to allow for more space when writing. There are enlarged checkbook registers and enlarged desk calendars and address books that can be purchased for minimal cost that will make it much easier for students with spatial problems to write more legibly and therefore be more organized.

Handwriting Strategies

Use a multisensory approach to teaching letter formation. Students with perceptual problems will have difficulty remembering how letters are formed, so when all of their senses are involved, they will have a better sense of the letter when they go to write it on paper. Try the following tactile approaches to teaching letter formation while having students say the letters aloud and describe their motions (e.g., "b goes down and around"). It is also helpful to have students practice forming groups of letters that have similar physical characteristics (e.g., "a, c, e, and o," or "m, n, and h").

- **Tactile Letters:** You can make or purchase sets of individual letters that are raised or textured in some way. Sandpaper letters are easy to make, as are raised letters made from dried Elmer's glue. Have students trace these letters with their fingers over and over while saying the letter at the same time.
- **Create large letters** on the floor and have students trace them by walking over the letters with their bodies. Students also enjoy trying to form the shape of letters while lying on the floor.

56

- **Have students write letters** in the air with their fingers, using large motions. Transfer this activity to writing imaginary letters on a wall (textured, if possible) and then on the back of a person standing in front of them and then onto their desk while they are sitting, and then onto a piece of paper. If they feel ready, they can then pick up a pencil and actually write the letter on the paper. Don't worry about staying in the lines at first. The students just need to get the feel of how the letter is formed and be able to translate that image from their minds to a piece of paper. Only when they can remember the letter formation with no difficulty should they start writing on and between lines.
- **Sandwriting:** Allow students to practice writing letters in textured material such as sand, salt, whipped cream, or chocolate pudding spread on a flat surface. Writing in sand placed in the lid of a shoebox is also an excellent way for older students to practice their spelling words.
- **Create opportunities** for letter formation. Students can write letters on the chalkboard or sidewalk, using water and a sponge or paintbrush. They can also form letters, using yarn, rope, clay, or pipe cleaners. Students also have great fun turning out the lights in the room and writing letters on the wall, using small flashlights or laser pointers.

Composition Strategies

- **Line-by-Line Writing:** Take a piece of lined paper and have the student write a complete thought on each line. This method will help the student develop the skill of writing complete thoughts. I use this method all the time. It helps me cut down on the amount of run-on sentences and fragments I tend to make. The teacher should review each sentence with the student to ensure that each is a complete thought. After a completed paragraph, have the student re-copy the sentences in paragraph form, plugging in the appropriate punctuation. Ideally, this process would be done on a computer, and recopying would not be necessary. This method provides a way for the student to develop individual thoughts without the clutter of other sentences or the pressure of putting in punctuation.

- **Note Taking:** Dyslexic writers are often unable to take notes and pay attention at the same time. In such cases, there are a variety of things that can help. An easy modification, and one that is often used in higher education, is to provide a note taker for the student. The note taker can use carbon or NCR paper in order to have an instant copy of their notes for the student, or copies can be made for the student on a copier. Teachers can also provide copies of their own notes for the student. This is particularly easy now with such presentation software as PowerPoint. In elementary classrooms, one of the goals is to teach students how to take notes, so it is important for dyslexic writers to practice this skill. However, if the student fails to correctly or completely copy down all the notes for a content course, it is likely that he or she will get behind in that subject area. In this case, the student should take notes along with everyone else, while another method is used to ensure that the student gets correct notes. The teacher can provide these directly to the student, privately, at a later time. Teachers who do not have time to make extra notes can provide NCR paper to another student in class and ask the student to make an extra set of notes, so the teacher will have a copy. This way, no one knows that the student with learning disabilities is getting a modification, thus avoiding embarrassment. Also, there are ways to take notes other than writing information in words. The dyslexic writer should be encouraged to experiment with taking notes in picture format, using graphic organizers, or by recording the notes on tape. The future of providing accessible notes for all students is moving toward web-based instructional curricula. Teachers place instructions, homework assignments, notes, and so forth, on a web site where students and parents can access it, making the material available to be used with adaptive software and hardware. There are also tape recorders that will translate auditory input directly into text. (See the technology section for further details.)

- **Topic Notecards:** Utilize index cards to help organize ideas before writing. Index cards come in a variety of colors and sizes, with and without lines. These cards allow the student to physically manipulate and organize his or her ideas before writing.

- **Sense of Audience:** As mentioned earlier, it is important to teach students to be aware of the audience to whom they are writing. Establishing the audience needs to be built into the prewriting discussion. Dyslexic writers should be encouraged to visualize the audience as they are writing. This can be an area of writing in which they excel.

- **Art Spelling:** Use art as a means to teach students to visualize their spelling words. Have students place spelling words in a collage or mosaic in a variety of colors. Be creative and keep in mind that spelling is a left-brain function. The more you can teach students to utilize the creative/visual right side of their brains, the better is the chance they will be able to recall difficult words later.

- **Tap into Students' Interests:** As discussed earlier in this chapter, it is important for students to practice writing—not a favorite activity for students with writing disabilities. The key is to find stimulating topics. At the beginning of the year, develop individualized student-interest sheets. These sheets highlight hotpoints of interest for individual students and can be used throughout the year to help stimulate the student's writing environment. It would be helpful not only to have broad topic areas of interest, but also to bullet-point reasons why these areas are of interest to the student. Keep in mind that interest areas change, so the sheet may need to be updated on a regular basis. Another technique to stimulate writing is class discussion. Through intense class discussion of literature that is read aloud to the class, dyslexic writers will have the opportunity to heighten awareness of the topic and formalize opinions, which will increase their interest and confidence in writing.

- **De-emphasize Mechanics:** Free up space. As a dyslexic writer, the mechanics of writing will always challenge me. Even though I have developed a true appreciation for good writing, I will never be able to create a piece of literature without utilizing specific writing accommodations and modifications. I have learned that the more I can de-emphasize the technical aspects of writing, the more creative and organized my thoughts become. De-emphasizing the mechanics reduces stress, anxiety, and frustration.
- **Utilize Strengths:** Tapping into students' learning strengths can help their writing process. Through movement and hands-on techniques, I am able to get my thoughts across in a logical and creative manner. Through utilizing my kinesthetic and tactile strengths, I am a more effective writer. It is important to tap into and use the individual student's learning style.
- **Dictation:** I know that dictation is a luxury that most students or adults with learning disabilities can't afford. However, during the student's initial development, I believe it is essential that he or she have one-on-one access to a tutor, parent, or peer student who can help organize and facilitate the teaching of effective writing. There are now voice-recognition systems that can help free up some of the mechanical difficulties a dyslexic writer may have. However, there is no substitute for a one-on-one writing-team approach in the beginning, when students are in the discovery process of developing composition styles that work best for them.
- **Graphic Organizers:** Graphic organizers are visual maps of a writing topic. Shapes and lines are used to connect the different sections of the topic. It is essential to develop and use these during the prewriting stage. They help students organize and understand the topic that is about to be written on. I use graphic organizers both when I'm writing and when I'm reading. They help connect my left and right

brains. There is no right or wrong way to create a graphic picture of a topic. Some students use simple lines to connect ideas, while others may draw elaborate pictures. The point is that the student thinks about and organizes the things he or she wants to say before the writing begins and has a visual picture to refer to as writing proceeds.

- **Color-code Parts of Speech:** Utilize color when introducing parts of speech. As you introduce and discuss nouns, verbs, pronouns, and so on, introduce them in a certain color. It is important to use the colors consistently. For example, if nouns are introduced in green, they should remain in green throughout the year and should appear in green when written on the board or on signs around the room. When students are asked to identify nouns from the board or on work sheets, they could underline or highlight the words in green. Using color is very helpful to dyslexic writers because of the difficulty they have differentiating between the parts of speech. They will learn to associate parts of speech with different colors and gradually learn to fade out the colors as they grow older. Color-coding the parts of speech will not work for students who are color-blind; however, the colors may be substituted with circles, squares, and other visual marks.

- **Individual Writing Boards:** Allow students to keep small writing boards at their desks. Encourage students to use these boards for brainstorming, graphic organizers, or practicing a word before writing it on paper. These boards can be a great way to jot down answers to questions that might be asked of them in class. These can also be used as response boards that students hold up in response to questions you ask the entire class. For example, to get children to practice recognition of the type of punctuation mark that goes at the end of a sentence, you can state sentences and have the students write the correct punctuation mark on the board and hold it up. You can immediately see which students are understanding and which students aren't. This works well for the dyslexic writer, because he or she is required to listen rather than read, and can participate in class with everyone else. Small dry-erase boards can be easily made from a large piece of tile board (sometimes called bathroom board), which can be purchased at hardware stores or home builders' supply companies.

- **Be Aware of Left-handers:** A high percentage of dyslexic writers are left-handed. Be aware of the classroom settings and materials that may make writing uncomfortable for these students. For example, many desks and notebooks are designed specifically for right-handed students. The best spiral-ring notebook is one that has the spiral rings at the top. If this is not available, allow the student to turn the spiral notebook upside down. Although three-ring binders can be used, left-handed students will have to remove the paper in order to write. This can create problems, because students are more likely to lose or disorganize their papers. If you require your students to use these binders, ask all students to remove their papers for written assignments and allow time at the end of lessons to help students return written materials to the notebooks in an organized manner. Also be sure to seat the left-handed student so that his or her arm does not hit another student's arm while writing.

- **Letters on the Desk:** There are commercialized alphabets available to be placed on individual desks. These can be very helpful for students who have trouble remembering how to form letters or remembering alphabetical order. Dyslexic writers sometimes have difficulty transferring images from the board to their paper, so having the letters close at hand is helpful.

- **Sign Language:** When teaching spelling, consider using sign language to help students anchor the letters in place. Sign language offers a kinesthetic, hands-on approach to helping students not only form the letters, but also sequence the letters. Some colleges and universities are accepting sign language as a foreign language requirement. Having a student take advantage of a sign language course may help him or her with a variety of future skills.

Four

An Elephant's Mind

When Rosemary and I came up with the title for this chapter, I could not get the profile out of my mind of a two-ton elephant with a little bitty pea brain lodged up in his big old head. Not knowing the theory behind why "elephants never forget," I am going to trust that either some man or woman came up with this theory based on research. I can just see some poor graduate assistant following an elephant around for a lifetime, recording his actions, just so all of us can sit around today and say that we wish we had memories like elephants. I learned early on that I was not blessed with the gift of having a steel-trap mind. My memory door operates on its own timeframe, only letting in bits and pieces of information. When information filters into my brain, it is not in any type of assembly-line format. Chunks of information pile into my brain and clog up the trapdoor so that when the door opens, the information that leaks in is out of order and full of holes. I know this is the case because I have been able to study first-hand the way my memory acts in different situations, such as school, work, and social settings. I have learned that my memory problems are due to my language-processing deficits. Memory is really organization—placing information in organized brain files, which can be easily found and pulled when needed. Because I have such difficulty processing written and spoken language, I'm either spending all of my energy trying to make sense of the words or just letting the words fly right by me. There is no time to organize the information for later retrieval. The majority of the time when I'm dealing with substantial information that I need to retain, the information just gets lost because my brain gets overloaded with the details of the language (e.g., the letters, sounds, combinations of words). For example, I have a hard time remembering what the title, Doctor of Philosophy (Ph.D.), stands for. The picture of a medical doctor immediately comes up, and then I get an image of couch counseling. Then I think, "No, that's a psychologist, not a philosopher . . . what does a philosopher look like?" The pictures don't merge until I am able to draw a connection between the two. The word *biofeedback* is another example. At first, this word makes no sense at all. I have no picture for *bio*. I can get a picture of a chicken eating his feed and then think of the word *back* as something bouncing back. It takes awhile to pull the words *feed* and *back* together, and *bio* remains lost forever. Trying to follow conversations is a challenge, so I rely heavily on the content of the sentence combined with voice tone, eye contact, and level of emphasis on the word. There is certainly no time to store the information in any type of manner for later retrieval. This method usually results in my getting the overall meaning of the sentence but losing the key terms used. Later, when I reflect on what was said or try to communicate about the subject with someone else, I am unable to do this effectively because I leave out the key words and phrases my brain was trying to dissect as I was trying to grasp the concept of the discussion.

One of the best ways for me to remember something—to keep the trapdoor open—is for the communicator to explain the concept in very general and broad terms, leaving specific details for later. For example, I can relate this to classroom learning by explaining the difficulty I had in Art History. Details such as an artist's name, the year of the painting, where it was painted, and what style of painting it was flashed on the screen before or along with the picture of the painting. These overwhelming details caused the painting to fly by. The most effective way for my brain to take in information is by painting the picture first through broad and general terms: the color, the texture, the way the strokes flow. Then I start adding the details slowly, drawing links between the details and the picture. Getting an overall feel for the painting allows me to better recall it from memory. Attaching a feeling to a work of art can also act as a springboard for the information to be recalled. For instance, if I view the painting as sad because of the dark colors and deeper brushstrokes, I am more likely to recall details about the painting later.

Understanding how my brain retains information is one of the most confusing aspects of my disability. With reading, writing, and math, I can see my mistakes. They are presented in front of me in black and white (and red ink). But with memory, it's different. When trying to recall facts, my brain operates on its own unique system, a system that is hard to grasp, yet affects me throughout my daily life. As an adult, I am keenly aware that this piece of my learning disability challenges my self-esteem more than any other aspect. I have fully accepted that I will always have difficulty reading, writing, and calculating figures, but it is difficult for me to accept my memory disability. I want to remember the name of the movie I saw with a friend last week. I want to be able to be actively involved in the topics that are discussed around the dinner table with friends. I want to be able to recall important details that affect my life. My memory problems are the one part of my disability that continues to take me back to the second and third grades, when I felt I couldn't do anything right. In order for me to be effective in my job, I use strategies that involve all my senses. I realize now that if these strategies had been put into place at an earlier age, I would have been able to retain more of what was presented to me in my academic coursework. Instead, I find myself backpedaling, trying to get hold of and tie together information that I should know. For example, many dinner conversations with friends revolve around topic areas such as history, religion, and politics. When I was presented with these subjects in school, I was never shown the big picture on these topics, so I had nothing to attach details to. At one of these dinners, the topic of "Watergate" came up. I listened to my friends volley facts back and forth that supported their opinions about current politics. Instinctively, I knew I was at a loss during this conversation, but I had an opinion and sided with one of my friends. However, without the ability to recall background information or read newspapers and newsmagazines, it was impossible for me to support my opinion. I kept quiet, much like I did in history class in school. Going home that night, I cursed myself for not being smarter. In my eyes, I had been neglected, which made me feel dejected, detached, and depressed. This is a daily occurrence in my life. It doesn't just happen around a dinner table. It bleeds into every aspect of my life. I have difficulty remembering the street where I live, the zip code I'm in, phone numbers, dates, hotels where I'm staying, cities I've visited, conferences where I've spoken, books I've listened to on tape, and radio shows I listen to every day. One of my gifts is the ability to organize, which de-emphasizes my memory problems. I prepare, prepare, prepare. In many situations, I can handle my memory deficit, but it is within the social and personal situations that I continue to fail.

In an effort to understand as much as I can about the brain and the way it functions, I read as much as possible about how the brain works. Most books on the brain are very complex and frustrating; I have learned through trial and error that the best books that contain basic information are written for children. One of my favorites is *The Brain* by Seymour Simon. He describes long- and short-term memory in the following way:

> Can you remember what you had for breakfast this morning? That's called short-term memory. Short-term memory has a very limited time span. You probably can't remember what you had for breakfast two weeks ago. But you can remember some things that happened to you months or even years ago, such as your first day at school. That's called long-term memory.
>
> An area in the front of the cortex seems to deal with short-term memory, while the rest of the cortex deals with both long- and short-term memories. Two narrow motor strips on either side of the cortex control muscles all over your body, such as those in

your lips, eyes, neck, thumbs and so on. Other areas of the cortex receive information from the skin, eyes, ears, nose, and taste buds. Still other areas are related to speech, learning, and thinking.

The actual memories seem to be stored in the chemicals found in nerve cells. One theory is that a change happens in the chemicals that relay nerve impulses. Another idea is that there is a change in the cells' internal chemistry, called RNA. Scientists are just beginning to find out how and where the brain stores memories and where thinking occurs. New discoveries about the brain are constantly being made, but many mysteries still remain. (Simon 1997, 26)

I have learned that the right side of the brain, or right hemisphere, is the place where music, artistic ideas, and the ability to understand shapes and forms lie. This side, the right side of my brain, is where I have the easiest time retaining information, because it is easy for me to visualize shapes and forms or set facts to rhythm. I am able to retain and recall this type of information more effectively. The right side of the brain is the right side for me. I have heard that left-handers use the right side of the brain more, whereas right-handers use the left side of the brain more. Most of my difficulties with language (reading, spelling, and forming correct sentences) are caused by problems in my left hemisphere. I visualize this as being a wide-open space, vacuous. It is dark, and I am searching for the letters, numbers, and signs to form the picture I need. But it is frustrating because this side of my brain knows no pictures. It only knows language. My attempts to connect the dots and form a picture fail as I struggle with decoding language. The only chance I have to gather the information I need to remember is to link the right side of my brain with my left side—to pull the two together by using effective strategies. If I want to remember an important fact that is language-based, I must reframe it into a visual and/or spatial image. This takes training and a lot of focused energy, as well as a teacher to help develop this technique.

One of the most difficult tasks I had to do in school was to memorize the states and capitals. Geography was a nightmare. Even though a picture of a map is very visual, the language got in the way and prevented me from learning the material. It wasn't until much later in my academic career that Rosemary taught me how to base memory on objects. Attaching facts to objects in the immediate surroundings made it possible for me to recall states and cities more accurately. Using my strength of memory for spatial information (a right-hemisphere function), we developed a method that allowed me to connect the states and cities on the map. I had the opportunity to use this method with a young student I was tutoring. We began by emptying the toy box and raiding the refrigerator to gather objects that would help jar his memory about each state. For example, we chose an orange to represent Florida, a Beanie Baby lobster to represent Maine, and a loaf of bread (wheat) to represent Kansas. Once we collected fifty objects, we placed them in the room in relation to where the states are on the map. I think teachers could easily do this in a classroom by having each student bring objects from home to represent assigned states. Then move all the desks out of the way and let them design their own U. S. map, using their objects. Rather than concentrating on letters or spatial representations on a two-dimensional map, creative learners can attach meaning to a physical form, which they can recall more easily. Attaching facts to physical objects works for all types of memorization. A bookcase with four shelves may stand for a fact with four points. For example, a student who is trying to remember the four major causes of the French Revolution might attach each cause to a shelf. Placing each cause on a shelf as he learns the information helps the student organize the information in a visual manner, which can be more easily recalled.

Even with these types of strategies, language can still be an obstacle. Just because I know where St. Louis, Missouri, is on a map doesn't mean I know how to spell it: hence the obstacle. In world geography, I had to learn countries and capitals of the world. Breaking the world map into continents, I began to use the same process as mentioned above. The problem came in reading, recognizing, and recalling the different countries and capitals by name. When learning the capital of England, I not only had to learn where it was located, but also the name, London. Attaching an object to the country on a map was easy (palace guard). Remembering the name *London* was harder. Putting an L on the guard's cap was a visual image that stuck. For the test, the teacher allowed me to have a word bank listing all the countries on one side of a page, with the countries on the other. I had to match the capitals with the countries and then locate them on a map. Because I could not read the word *London*, I had to rely on the right side of my brain to memorize the form and feeling of "London" in order to match it up with England. In using this technique, I look at the word as if it's an amoeba, focusing on the first letter of the word and the way the amoeba hugs the letters. My goal is to be able to recognize the first letter and remember the form of the word. In doing this, I am able to retain where the letter L and its amoeba (shape) is located on the map. The problem comes when there are two or more capitals that start with the same letter. This is when it is vital that I rely on each individual amoeba, and hope that there are few L words. This is how I connect the left and right brain.

This works for a test. However, in a social situation, it's a different story. Even though I put all this effort into memorizing this information for a test, I cannot count on it sticking years later. The goal of teachers working with students who have language difficulties should be to teach a long-lasting understanding of a concept, making an effort to help the student organize information so that it stays with him or her over the long haul. I spent many years of my educational career using a Band-Aid approach to learning. I spent hours memorizing minute details, which I forgot immediately following the test. I wish I had had more time to spend on developing an informed, "big picture" view of a topic that would rest in my long-term memory.

I have focused on memory strategies for students with a strong right brain. What if the student is the opposite and has good language skills but difficulty with spatial and visual processing? Students with these difficulties will not have as much trouble learning the names of countries, states, and capitals as they will remembering where they are located on a map. When they see a map, the shapes and forms have little meaning; all they can see are the words. The left side of their brains make a verbal connection, but the right side has difficulty creating an accurate visual image. To look at this another way, if I were traveling through England, I would look for pictures and be the driver of a car, whereas my counterpart would have no problem reading the words (signs) but would have difficulty visualizing where he or she was in the country and perhaps would be unable to drive because of the spatial difficulties in adjusting to a different way of driving. A person with visual spatial deficits would have a much easier time learning the facts about a country than locating the country on a map. Teachers might help these students by creating a map with textured surfaces and by giving verbal descriptions of the items on the map. These students will excel in multiple-choice tests about countries but would be expected to have less success with map tests. Instead of having to take map tests, they may be given the modification of taking tests in which verbal descriptions of the countries are given rather than visual representations. This allows these students to use their left hemisphere to remember information usually processed by the right hemisphere, connecting the left brain with the right brain.

According to Howard Gardner, a pioneer in the contemporary understanding of multiple intelligences, "intelligence refers to the human ability to solve problems or make something that is valued in one or more cultures"(Checkley 1997). Gardner theorizes that there are at least eight ways by which the human brain approaches these tasks. He calls these multiple intelligences the "Eight Ways of Knowing." Each of the Eight Ways of Knowing may be considered a way of making meaning or "comprehending" visual or oral text.

Gardner's Eight Ways of Knowing is a very popular concept in education today, but how does it relate to students with learning disabilities? The goal of this book is to expose teachers to strategies that can help improve the quality of education for their students who learn differently. Because these individuals are placed in all types of school settings, I feel that it is important to use a theory such as Gardner's in order to examine ways that creative learners can learn more effectively. Both Rosemary and I believe Gardner's Eight Ways of Knowing complement the unique learning styles of students with learning disabilities, and I have found that Gardner's ideas have given me a perfect foundation for developing new ways to store and retrieve information. The following Eight Ways of Knowing are presented from my personal perspective as a learner:

1. *Linguistics:* This way of knowing is the ability to use language to express what is on your mind and to understand other people. First of all, let's look at the word *linguistics* from the perspective of a person with a verbal deficit. The word itself does not lend itself to a "warm, fuzzy" feel. My struggles with language involve a thin dictionary of vocabulary words to pull from. I have had to learn how to express myself articulately through a handful of carefully chosen words. In order for me to add words to this thin dictionary, it takes a lot of effort and role playing in order to save them in my memory banks. Because most schools rely heavily on linguistics in order to teach and test their students, many students with language deficits fail. I now understand the art of linguistics. Through my public speaking and my major in rhetorical speaking, I can appreciate the art of language. Even though I will never be a great orator (thanks, Rosemary, for this word), I will always strive to thicken my dictionary. However, children should not have to struggle to learn. As a teacher, please don't rely on language as your primary teaching tool. For students who do learn well linguistically, activities such as having them write in journals, create oral or written imaginative stories, and writing poetry are excellent activities.

2. *Logical/Mathematical:* This way of knowing is most often associated with scientific problem solving or inductive and

deductive reasoning. Most standardized tests are made up of information that requires either linguistics or this logical/ mathematical way of knowing. This explains why I did so poorly on all of those standardized tests growing up. Maybe this is why I have questioned so many of the IQ scores of people I work with who also have learning disabilities. One of the primary assumptions about a person with a learning disability is that his or her brain perceives information differently. For example, if I am reading a sentence, my perception of the words may be inaccurate because of visual discrimination problems, and I may process the words in a different order than they are written because of my syntax deficits. If the information is not being perceived accurately, it cannot be processed in an organized manner. For students who do learn well this way or who need practice in this way of thinking, have them practice outlining techniques and justifying answers to "How" and "Why" questions.

3. *Visual/Spatial:* This way of knowing refers to a strong sense of visual and spatial awareness. As is discussed throughout this book, this is a learning method I can rely on. Through visualization, I am able to organize information in a way I can remember. Relying on a good sense of where I am in space helps me organize my life. I have good time-management skills and have little difficulty navigating without a map, simply relying on visual objects placed along the way. However, there are people in my learning disabilities adult support group who struggle with visual/spatial information. Some have difficulty driving, following and giving directions, or even telling time. In one instance, a member in his mid-forties came up to me and told me that it took him six years to get to the support group meeting. When I questioned him about this, he relayed to me that over the last six years, every time he attempted to come to a meeting, he got lost and would give up and go home. For students who have strengths in this area, however, learning could be made so much easier if they had the opportunity to process new in-

formation or demonstrate learned concepts through visual/ spatial learning activities. One such activity was discussed earlier when I described learning the location of the fifty states by creating my own map, with objects representing each state. I would have given anything in school if teachers would have allowed me to demonstrate my knowledge of a subject by creating a sculpture or a painting or a photographic essay rather than writing a ten-page paper.

4. *Bodily Kinesthetic:* This way of knowing refers to the ability to use the body or parts of the body to solve a problem or retain information. The primary way I tackle information is through a kinesthetic approach. This approach has been known to work particularly well with actors, dancers, or athletes. Using the body to take in and store information is a natural way for me to learn. Whether I study by running around the track or washing my hair, the information sticks in a retrievable order in my brain. In college I learned to use kinesthetic learning in every medium of academics. When writing, I find it most effective to express myself when I am moving around and dictating my thoughts. When reading, I comprehend the material better if I am standing and/or walking backwards. I seem to have the ability to scan words on a page more effectively when I am moving. Walking backwards while reading de-emphasizes the anxiety I usually feel when looking at the printed page. I am more concerned about falling on my butt than about reading the words, which is an unusual feeling in someone who struggles with reading. When memorizing a fact, it helps to toss or juggle something in my hands. The combination of all these kinesthetic methods drives me closer to academic success. To promote bodily kinesthetic learning in the classroom, teachers can use role playing, drama, or other types of movement activities, such as having students spell out words by using their bodies.

5. *Musical/Rhythmic Intelligence:* I have always wondered if reading music was anything like reading print. I know that I have often used music to learn new information; however, I think it

is that I want to move when I hear music, and it's the movement that really helps me learn. For example, I learned to sound out syllables in words by pounding them out on the kitchen table with my grandmother, who would form the syllables into a short melody. I do think the rhythm of the activity helped, but it was probably the physical pounding that helped most. The combination of the music and the movement offered an anchor for my brain to grab on to. My difficulty with this type of learning lies in my auditory-processing difficulties. Just as I can't hear the difference in similar sounding letters, I have difficulty hearing an entire range of pitches. The bottom line is that learning with music is fun and promotes a positive atmosphere for learning. In addition, research on the brain and learning has documented the importance of music in brain development. A survey of studies suggests that music plays a significant role in enhancing a wide range of academic and social skills. James Hanshumacher (1980) reviewed thirty-six studies and concluded that arts education facilitates language development, enhances creativity, boosts reading readiness, helps social development, assists general intellectual achievement, and fosters positive attitudes toward school. At the very least, music is a language that can enhance the abilities of children who don't excel in the expression of verbal thinking. You can't beat that!

6. *Interpersonal:* This way of knowing refers to an individual's ability to understand other people, work cooperatively in a group, and/or communicate verbally and nonverbally with other people. This type of learning can be difficult to grasp for an individual with learning disabilities because, in order to survive in an academic and social setting, individuals with learning disabilities use an exorbitant amount of energy on developing their own survival (manipulation) skills in order to get through their day-to-day lives. Interpersonal intelligence entails being actively involved with and aware of other people, and learning from their perspectives. Sometimes, individuals with learning disabilities become so self-absorbed

74

in their own struggle for survival that they develop narcissistic qualities that make it difficult to develop interpersonal ways of learning. For instance, students with learning disabilities sometimes fail to consider the needs or feelings of the teachers or tutors they depend on for help. They may wait until the last second to ask a teacher for test modifications or may blame the teacher for "not teaching the material right" when they fail. This often happens in college settings when students won't meet with the professor at the beginning of a semester but wait until their grades are in jeopardy before making professors aware of needed accommodations. If students with learning disabilities could learn to utilize each other's strengths and weaknesses to build a cooperative team approach, lessons would become more interesting and interactive. Teachers can encourage the development of interpersonal skills by setting up opportunities for cooperative learning in the classroom (e.g., allowing groups or teams of students to work together on projects, presentations, or test preparation). One of the best ways for me to learn is through a discussion group. It allows me to hear the perspective of the subject matter from several angles. Today, when sitting in meetings, I use interpersonal learning in order to gather information I may miss in written documents.

7. *Intrapersonal:* This way of knowing refers to people's understanding of themselves, or self-awareness. This type of learning can be very powerful in the classroom. Tapping into personal subject matter can have very positive outcomes in learning. For example, one of the most effective ways for me to learn is to draw connections between the subject matter and a personal experience. The most obvious example I could give is my advocacy work in the field of learning disabilities. Because of my passion for helping students with learning disabilities, I am continuously learning about this subject by examining and reflecting on my own personal experiences. This subject matter (learning disabilities) can be broken into many areas, including workplace issues, social

issues, and medical issues, all of which I can relate to my personal experiences with learning disabilities, thereby opening windows to even more areas of learning. My first memory of using intrapersonal learning was fifth grade, when I first experienced the taste of success through swimming. After a year of receiving ribbons and medals in the pool, I began to adapt the same philosophy I had on the pool deck to the classroom. If hard work, determination, and drive worked for me in the pool, I reasoned that maybe they could also work for me in the classroom. Giving up was not an option; this philosophy rang true and clear from my coaches. I became a better student. Teachers can assist their students in this process by helping them explore their strengths outside the classroom, asking questions, and connecting learning to the students' personal interests.

8. *Naturalist:* This way of knowing refers to the human ability to discriminate among living things as well as demonstrate a sensitivity to features of the natural world. This type of learning is hard for me to grasp; however, I can relate to it because I am familiar with the ecosystem and how it plays out in our everyday life. Drawing on nature in order to educate students can be a very familiar and logical way of learning. Nature is something that one personally experiences every day and is easy to draw connections to. I remember, in geography class, learning the difference between a cumulus cloud and a nimbus cloud. Even though I have difficulty with the language of nature, I am still able to physically experience clouds. Because of my personal exposure to clouds, it was much easier for me to learn their names and characteristics. Teachers often miss the opportunity to use the best classroom of all—nature.

Gardner stresses the importance of providing opportunities for students to use all Eight Ways of Knowing. For example, if a teacher were trying to teach the skeletal system, he or she would prepare activities that incorporate each of the Eight Ways of Knowing. The class might begin by attaching words and definitions to a diagram of Johnny the Skeleton, who is falling apart. Johnny becomes real as the students develop a poem that describes Johnny and his bones from head to toe. Working together as a whole class or even in teams, the class gives Johnny a personality, drawing on their own real-life experiences (intrapersonal), which utilizes their interpersonal skills but, more importantly, gives Johnny a "life." Adding music to Johnny's journey (poem), Johnny becomes an active part of the class. As Johnny develops a life, gestures are added to describe and locate different bones. A skit might be developed around Johnny the Skeleton, who is falling apart, and with help from his friends, gets put back together bone by bone (emphasizing the spatial relationships of the bones to each other and how they fit together). The skit concludes with a systematic count of all the bones to make sure Johnny is whole (logical/mathematical). The students will relate personally to Johnny and might even explore the cycle of life and death as it relates to nature.

Even though I have been aware of my memory disability for the last couple of years, it still puzzles me how it affects me in all those different settings: work, personal, and social. As I mentioned earlier in this chapter, it is the one part of my disability that I truly struggle to grasp, and at this time in my life it is the one part of my disability that continues to pull my self-esteem down. I have learned to intentionally surround myself with people who understand my disability in some small way and, more importantly, who know my capabilities. Surrounding myself with positive friends and adding techniques and strategies that help me stay on task have been the keys to my success. Some of these daily strategies I use I have learned on my own or have borrowed from other people. Many of my strategies involve technology. For example, I use an electronic organizer to keep phone numbers and addresses in. I have personally selected one that has an auto-dialer built in that dials the numbers for me without my having to struggle through punching them in. I have a spiral-ring index card notebook with lines, which allows me to keep track of all the things I need to do that I can't transpose into my personal organizer. I keep a stack of yellow sticky notes on my bathroom counter, which provide me a way to draw pictures (notes) of things I need to do. I place them on the mirror so that I see them first thing every morning. I have a small voice memo recorder on the refrigerator that I am able to speak into to help me keep a grocery list and to remind me of other household errands I need to run. I've learned to use my phone voice mail to leave messages for myself. If I am away from home or my office, I'll call my home voice mail and leave myself messages.

In addition to these tools, I use a combination of the Eight Ways of Knowing in order to get information into my mind in a retrievable order. For example, if I have to memorize a lot of steps taken in the completion of a project, I put on a blindfold to help me visualize the step-by-step process the project took. The blindfold buffers out outside stimuli and allows me to visualize in my mind the clear and distinct steps the project has taken. It's a wonderful strategy that I learned from my swim coach, who used to blindfold us as we were swimming the back stroke to help us visualize where we were in the pool and to help us focus on the number of strokes we were taking from one end of the pool to the other.

In a recent project for work, it was my job to update an advisory board on the legislative process our technology resource centers had gone through in order to obtain additional funding. Knowing that this process would be very difficult for me to talk about, I started using some memory strategies to help me get a clear picture of the process. Blindfolding allowed me to visualize the funding request going from the House to the Senate and back to the House. I actually visualized with the blindfold a piece of paper, which represented our request, with legs walking from one place to the other. I added earplugs to help further block out the noise and help me concentrate on the process. After I literally walked through the whole process, I would take the blindfold off and graph out the process on paper, using different sizes and shapes of boxes, lending the larger sizes to the most important issues. Going back and forth from the paper to the blindfold, I eventually was able to make the process stick, and when it became my time to recall it, not only did I have a full visual picture of the process, I was also able to doodle the graphic illustration.

In working with adolescents and adults with learning disabilities, it is apparent to me that people have different levels of difficulty with organization and memory. My difficulty with memory lies in my inability to process language effectively. However, there are others who struggle with organizing their day-to-day activities in an effective manner. What do you do when you wake up in the morning? What organizational format do you use throughout your day to get from one place to another? These simple tasks are major problems for people with severe organizational or memory problems. It is vital that a system be put into place that includes clear and easy directions to follow.

In many cases, the adults I have worked with have had to learn this process on their own through trial and error. It would have been so much easier for them if they had had explicit instruction in organizational/memory techniques at an earlier age. It is a common feeling to be very frustrated with these individuals. Their lack of organization can step on every nerve in your body, and they are usually the students who seem to miss out on the whole picture of a school day, not quite getting the transition from class to class or class to lunch or recess. Change is very difficult for them, and everyone loses patience with them. I worked with one student who could not get a clear picture of her class schedule and what she needed to do throughout the day to get from one place to the other. This specific case opened my eyes for the first time to how my disability looks to other people. Because I have good time-management skills, it was very hard for me to relate to and understand this student's inability to organize her day. I could tell right from the beginning that she was clueless and scared about the transitions she had to make throughout the day, so when I found myself getting frustrated with her, I put myself in her shoes, and we systematically designed a step-by-step process for her to go to class, then to her locker, then to another class, back to her locker, then on to lunch. We did this using two different methods. The first was a color-coded, paper-trail outline of her schedule. Her locker was always Home Base. She kept the diagram of her schedule in her notebook and in her locker. Home Base (locker) was always color-coded in red. Classes were color-coded in blue. The cafeteria and gym were in different colors. At the beginning of learning the strategy, she always returned to Home Base to get her bearings. Other strategies that I used with her were a voice organizer, which would tell her at the end of each class where she was supposed to go next. Another strategy we tried, but which did not work as well, was having her carry around a beeper that beeped or vibrated when it was time to be at the next class. Watches with alarms can do the same function. Although neither of these worked with her, they may work well for other students.

It is important, when working with students with severe memory/organization problems, that you don't assume the obvious. To most people, it is just natural to understand and follow a daily schedule. With these individuals, that is not the case, and it is important that you go back to the beginning and break down the process, whether it is a daily schedule or a complicated school assignment. If teachers start working with students at an early age to develop compensatory techniques such as these, then these students' adult lives will be much more manageable.

Works Cited

Checkley, K. 1997. "The First Seven . . . and the Eighth: A Conversation with Howard Gardner." *Education Leadership* 55 (1): 8–13.

Hanshumacher, J. 1980. "The Effects of Arts Education on Intellectual and Social Development: A Review of Selected Research." *Bulletin of the Council for Research in Music Education* 61(2): 10–28.

Simon, S. 1997. *The Brain.* New York: Morrow Junior Books.

Five

Just Add Water

The vans followed each other closely up I-85 North to Dynamo Swim Center in Atlanta. The windows, steamed over from body heat, became our billboards:

"PJC kicks butt!"
"Distance swimmers do it longer"
"Backstrokers do it on their backs"

Such was the boasting of the Pensacola Junior Team on our way to the first big meet of the year, and my first big meet ever. Towels still damp from our pre-trip swim were slung over the backs of bucket seats; musky gym bags packed with swim suits, goggles, Walkmen, Jell-O packets for energy, school books, and cards crowded the floor under our restless feet. I sat anxiously in the rear seat, anticipating my turn on the starting block. A part of me was full of pride; I had made the traveling team (they needed me!), and it felt good. I was part of a group, I was wanted for something I was pretty good at, and I was waiting to prove it. It was 1979, and my favorite song was blaring over the adolescent chatter.

This was a new experience for me in more ways than one. I had always been set apart before for being different, for not being smart enough to remain in class with my peers. My learning disabilities consigned me to special classes away from the others. When I was tested in the second grade, the diagnosis indicated that I would always have difficulty in school, and there was little expectation that I would improve. But here I was, Walkman in hand, staring at Atlanta's incessant road construction and visualizing a good start, a strong swim, and a great finish. This time I would not disappoint my coach (teacher) or my teammates (classmates). I was thirteen, a gawky age at best, but for the first time, I felt like I belonged.

———————

For several years now, parents, teachers, and administrators have asked me for my secret of success. How did I develop the motivation and intellectual abilities to get through the academic system? My answer is simply, "I just added water." I attribute my academic success to swimming, a sport I threw myself into in the fifth grade. As I think back to what this sport provided me, I am aware of its awesome influence on my entire life. Swimming became the medication I needed for my learning disability. With every dose I took, I got stronger. My motivation for life developed and my learning improved. I have always been aware of the impact swimming has had on my self-esteem, but it has not been until the last couple of years that I have comprehended how swimming tied into my academic achievement.

Some of my favorite childhood memories are of being pushed higher and higher in a swing by another child or being spun faster and faster on a playground merry-go-round. It saddens me that, because of liability issues, swings and merry-go-rounds are beginning to disappear from playgrounds across the country. Sometimes I get the feeling that society is so concerned about preventing lawsuits that they are depriving students of the opportunity to play. I am also aware that recess time, along with art, music, and physical education, are the first things to be cut when money is tight or when there is a push to have students spend more time in the classroom on academics. I can't tell you the number of times I've been told by parents that they are planning to take their child out of a physical activity because his or her grades are low. In a 1995 *U. S. News & World Report* article, Brink reported that 64 percent of K–12 American students do not participate in a daily physical education program. At the present time, over 50 percent of children ride a school bus to school rather than walk. The average child in the United States sits in front of a television for six to eight hours a day. Even children's sports, which were daily and self-organized in the 1950s, have been replaced by organized sports run by adults, in which sitting on the bench far exceeds the time playing (Putnam and Copans 1998).

In his book, *Teaching with the Brain in Mind*, Eric Jensen (1998) makes the point that in the same way that exercise shapes up the muscles, heart, lungs, and bones, it also strengthens the basal ganglia, cerebellum, and corpus callosum, all key areas of the brain. In fact, Jensen reports a large amount of research that links brain development and academic achievement to movement. It makes common sense to me that kinesthetic and tactile classroom activities can only improve the students' academic success. I may be biased because kinesthetic learning is *the* most effective way for information to get into and be processed by my brain. The lessons I learned the most from in school were wrapped around activities that involved movement. For instance, as one might guess, I was no fan of spelling bees; however, one of my teachers held a different kind of bee. She cut out letters and taped them to the blackboard and then had competing students come to the board to place the letters in the correct spelling of a word. The class was designed to be in a relaxed format. Students were able to stand by their desks or even lean against the wall. This was the first and only time I can remember being intrigued about how letters were placed in order to make up a word. I am sure this positive experience was due to the movement involved in the activity. Physically manipulating the letters brought a sense of control to me, and because of the movement, the letters seemed to stick longer in my brain.

Another example of when my grades started to improve due to movement was when I developed a study technique of reviewing and memorizing information as I swam lap-to-lap in practice. I vividly remember days in the eighth grade, coming home from school and reviewing the notecards my tutor had made for me to study for a test. The question was on one side, and the answer was on the other. These notecards were easy for me to use. They were portable and fit easily into my swimbag. As I traveled to practice, I would review the cards. When practice started and we were given a long, mundane swim set, the notecards would visually pop up in my head, and I would start reviewing them. The time I spent in the pool became my own private classroom. It didn't matter if the set involved kicking, pulling, or lap-to-lap swimming; my brain grabbed hold of the subject matter and dissected it until I understood the content. This pool time was also valuable from an organizational standpoint. I found it much easier to organize my thoughts as I swam. This did not work well when I was involved with other teammates, doing relays or some other type of team activity. It worked the best when I had little contact with other swimmers. I truly believe that team sports are important, but when it comes to learning, the best activity is one that involves individual movement with little interpersonal contact.

"One, two, three," I counted, my right hand on my left shoulder. Three swings forward, then three swings back. The same again, right arm. I had done this a million times before. My arms felt rubbery. I was tapered and shaved. The water was cool and deep, perfect for racing. I stepped up onto the block, angled and rough, just right. Orange and blue lane ropes stretched the length of the pool. Twenty-five yards to my first turn. I glanced up at the scoreboard. I visualized my race, the time. I had done this, too, before. But this time was different. This was my last race, the last time I would compete for the University of Georgia. I had done it, made it to this final race. Thirteen years, to be exact, swimming day after day to reach this moment. My goggles in place, I waited for the start.

"Swimmers, take your mark." A deep breath in, a slow exhale, a peaceful place. "Beep." The water felt just right, my follow-through, strong; my head, high; the wall, in front of me. First flip turn. I streamline. Second turn, kick harder. Third turn, head up, sprint. Three good turns. Reaching for the finish, I was on my last lap. Stroke after stroke I glided through the water, swimming through the pain. I finished. It was over, my arms and legs trembling as I escaped from the pool.

———————

Looking back on that period of time in my life, I now realize how important it was for me to have my coach's approval. He was my teacher, a teacher who would not take "no" for an answer. There would be no victims in his pool, only winners. Even though winning was important, it was not number one on the list. My teammates and I were expected to give 100 percent, no questions asked. We became machines in the water, able to take on any set (problem). The phrase, "I can't," was not in our vocabularies.

Jensen (1998) makes the point that "in sports, we expect learners to use their brains for counting, planning, figuring, and problem-solving. Every athlete is highly engaged in cognitive functions. It makes sense that we'd expect students to use their bodies for kinesthetic learning in the academic classes" (35). It is my observation that coaches can get away with doing more with their athletes than teachers can do with their students. There seems to be some unspoken law that says coaches have the right to expect high levels of achievement no matter what it takes, whereas teachers are confined to four classroom walls and a curriculum dictated by the state. I am convinced that in order to tap into the mind of creative learners, the school doors must be unlocked so that the students can learn in an environment that best fits their learning styles.

I am aware that some students may not feel comfortable with kinesthetic learning. In fact, individuals with nonverbal learning disabilities have difficulties with spatial perception and coordination, so they may have true difficulties with movement exercises. However, research in brain-based learning indicates that there are simple movement exercises, which can be incorporated into any classroom, that will benefit all learners. For those who are kinesthetic learners, just a little bit of freedom to move around in the classroom may make a world of difference in their ability to learn and retain new information.

Tips for Teachers

Stretching

Just as you would stretch before you run, it is also helpful for students to stretch before they start learning. Simple neck, arm, and leg stretches can help students focus and get their juices flowing. One way to achieve relaxation and reduction of anxiety is to have students concentrate on a body part and tense it up for five to ten seconds and then relax it; then continue to do this with other body parts. Stretching should be used before, during, and after intense academic work. Some teachers fear that it would be hard to maintain control of the classroom using this type of exercise; however, if you develop an organized group stretching routine, you will be surprised how well your students take to it. Making this a regular part of the day will de-emphasize class disruption. You might want to ask the PE teacher at your school or another exercise specialist to help you design a very easy and short stretching program if you do not feel comfortable doing this yourself.

Expressive Walking

One of the most effective ways for kinesthetic learners to get information into their heads is by simply standing up and being allowed to walk around the room without restriction. Of course, this needs to be done during appropriate times. Students need to understand that they cannot disrupt the teacher or their classmates. This is their own personal learning strategy, for which they need to take responsibility. Walking around will help kinesthetic learners in organizing their thoughts, memorizing content, and expressing their ideas. As I am writing this book this very moment, I am pacing and dictating my thoughts and words to Rosemary. When I am sitting in a chair, the words don't come. Allowing your students to move will allow them to problem-solve through motion.

Expressive Gesturing

For many kinesthetic learners, it comes naturally to express their thoughts through body language. Watch your students to see if they have a tendency to use gestures when articulating an idea or thought. Hand gestures and other nonverbal body communication can be a wonderful way for students to organize their thoughts as well as express their ideas. Use of appropriate body gestures should be encouraged and brought to the attention of the student. I have learned through watching tapes of myself speaking to audiences that I am most effective when using hand and body gestures. I have been amazed at the amount of information I can get across to people by using gestures when my verbal expression fails.

Jumping Rope

Use jump ropes in the classroom when appropriate. They can be particularly effective for test review, or they can simply be offered as a reward for a job well done. For example, if you have enough jump ropes for the entire class, go outside on nice days and jump rope while shouting out the multiplication facts, the presidents of the United States, or any other topic that needs continuous repetition for learning. If you only have a few jump ropes, divide the class into groups and ask each individual a question for test review. If the question is answered correctly, the student can use the jump rope to jump to an established point and back. Or divide the class into several teams and ask them sets of questions. At the end of the game, the two winning teams can use (a sturdy) jump rope to have a tug-of-war to establish the final winning team. All of these activities get students out of their desks and into a new learning environment where they have room to move around while they learn.

Moving Math

Math is one of those subjects that is easier to teach when movement is involved. Measurement can easily be taught by having students measure everything in the room. Helping students understand the need for standard measurements can be easily demonstrated by having students measure objects with their hands, fingers, arms, feet, and so forth, and discovering that no two students will come up with the same measurement. Teaching beginning learners how to form numbers is so much easier if the students have the opportunity to form the numbers with their bodies as they learn. Having students line up two by two, three by three, and so on, helps them get the concept of grouping, which can be applied to multiplication, division, and fractions. Students will learn numeration and place value much easier if you let them become numbers and experience the changes as they move from one place value to another.

Playing Catch

Use a lightweight ball or a nerfball in the classroom to get students up and moving for a variety of activities. The person with the ball asks a question and then throws it to another person to answer. "Hot Potato" is another game that can easily be used for test review or repetitious activities. The ball is passed quickly around until the teacher signals, and whoever has the ball must answer a question. This is a great activity for a rainy day, when the students have to stay inside. Teach students how to juggle, and challenge them to do this while reciting a poem or multiplication tables, the five Great Lakes, the Thirteen Colonies, and so forth.

Calisthenics/Arm Raises

Calisthenics can be used to wake up endorphins and increase students' levels of alertness. When students seem to be tired or overwhelmed with information, stop the class and have everyone do jumping jacks, push-ups, or sit-ups.

Cadence

Follow the example of the military, which has used movement for years in the education of their troops. Whether used for marching, calisthenics, or drills, military movement is always performed to a cadence. To this day, I remember the summer between my sixth and seventh grades, when I attended a Catholic summer school. As much as I hated being there, I did learn a tremendous amount and still retain some of those things today. This is because most of the subjects were taught to us as a team, using a cadence. In a united rhythm, we would recite information aloud while marching in pairs outside around the track.

Silly Putty or Grip Ball

This is a very nonobtrusive way for students to move at their desks. These objects can relieve stress for the students or allow them to release stored energy so that they may focus on the task at hand.

Tactile Learning

A smaller form of kinesthetic learning is tactile. This refers to touching or using a hands-on approach to learning. Tactile learning can be used in all subject matters. Something as simple as following along printed lines of material with your finger as you read can make it easier to follow and comprehend the material. Building a model is another very effective hands-on approach to learning, which not only develops patience, but also the ability to sequentially think through a problem. Art classes are a wonderful way for students to experience a variety of tactile methods of learning; the key is to help teachers learn to apply these methods to academics. For instance, if you are learning about the Industrial Revolution, painting or drawing a picture of the time period will help the students place themselves in that setting.

Conclusion

When working with individuals with learning disabilities, it is important to keep in mind that they do not learn in a traditional manner. Their brains are "wired" differently. For me, the answer was to "just add water," but a solution is never that simple. Teachers, students, and parents must work together to find techniques that work. Because so many creative learners find success in the areas of athletics (Greg Louganis, Bruce Jenner, Magic Johnson) and creative arts (Cher, Henry Winkler, Tracy Gold), where movement and learning go hand in hand, it makes sense to me that kinesthetic learning techniques would be well worth trying in the classroom.

Works Cited

Brink, S. May 15, 1995. "Smart Moves." *U. S. News & World Report.*
Jensen, E. 1998. *Teaching with the Brain in Mind.* Alexandria, VA: Association for Supervision and Curriculum Development (ASCD).
Putnam, S., and Copans, S. A. 1998. "Exercise: An Approach to the Treatment of ADHD." *Reaching Today's Youth: The Community Circle of Caring Journal* 2:66–68.

Six

Charms: Honoring the Student's Personal Survival Strategies

Smoke and Mirrors

I Know You.
I have to Know You
I Know what makes You
smile—
laugh—
enraged—
weep.
I Know what makes You stop
and think.
I've been the Jane Goodall
of this place
for as long
as I have
been
here.
I must Know
and understand
YOU . . .
My survival is undeniably linked
to this Know-Ledge
And No . . .
You don't Know me . . . at all.
　　　　　　　　—Carolyn Phillips

A feeling of anguish comes over me as I enter the hallowed halls of school. Being keenly aware of everything around me, I proceed down the hallway, taking in minute details and storing them for later. You see, it is my job to make note of the little details around me. Perception is my sword in this fantasyland. Survival is my goal. I learned early on to master my gifts in order to survive in a land in which I neither belong nor understand. I am aware that the battlefield I step on to everyday is designed to catch me in my mistakes. I am very gifted in the art of manipulation. Like a thief, my job is to trick the enemy into giving me what I want. No matter how much I prepare every night before coming to this battlefield, it never seems to be enough, so I have no choice but to rely on my bag of charms, calling on them when I find myself in desperate situations, fighting the enemy. My charms work in most difficult situations. At times, they are able to get me out of situations where I might have to read aloud, or even more importantly, they allow me to vanish before spelling bees. These charms do not work alone. Combined with the minute details I gather throughout the day, the charms glimmer as they get me out of one desperate situation after another.

Teachers have little difficulty recognizing them: the identities that students take on in the classroom. There is the Class Clown, the Bully, the Troublemaker, the Shy Kid, the Teacher's Pet, and the Eager Beaver. It's an identifiable behavior that students use to get what they want. I always thought of these personal behaviors as charms; they were pieces of magic I could use at will to help me get through each day of school. Many students with learning disabilities are masters of manipulating situations to get what they need. While these charms may work well in the short term, over a period of time their use may become detrimental to learning and character development.

One of the most difficult daily tasks for me as an adult is looking up information, whether it is a phone number, a word definition, or Internet information. It has taken me years to undo what my charms provided me access to as a child. Due to my difficulties with academics, combined with my low self-esteem, I was determined to get out of every challenge presented to me by sounds, symbols, and language. I wanted nothing to do with even simple tasks that were difficult for me. Even writing down my swimming events and times on my Deck Entry Cards brought anxiety-producing stress. I became oblivious to my friends as they sat around rattling off important cut-off times. There was never a break; I could never rest. Everywhere I looked, I was surrounded by sounds, symbols, and written information. The environment was overwhelming for a warrior who only had charms to rely on.

As President of LD Adults of Georgia, one of the strongest LD adult organizations in the country, I have spent the last few years surrounded by adults with learning disabilities—the mature product of our public school system. It has been some of the most rewarding but challenging work in my life. It has made me realize that not everyone with learning disabilities uses charms in the same way that I do. Many people get what they want by nagging, whining, and bullying their teachers, parents, and friends. At first I did not see through the facade of these individuals. I found myself upset with the coping skills they had learned early on to get through the system. Like everyone else, I only saw the Whiner, the Nagger, or the Bully. As I worked more closely with these individuals, I discovered that what they were doing was not that much different from what I have done all my life to survive. However, instead of nagging or whining when something doesn't go my way, I become complacent with things around me. As I ventured through the education system, I learned not to care too deeply about any one view. I found myself agreeing and disagreeing on the same topics, unwilling to form any one opinion, always bouncing back to the middle. I was Mr. Stretch in the cartoon series, *The Fantastic Four*, able to take everything, no matter how hard it was, and stretch back to my original form. Through school I stayed focused on getting from grade to grade, not caring about what I learned or anything else. I strictly focused on one test after the other, paying little attention to learning the content of the subject, but simply about whether or not I received a passing grade.

Even though I studied hard every night and did everything the teachers suggested, I was always aware that I would only get to the edge of passing. In order to make sure I got that passing grade, I utilized every charm in my bag of tricks. The best word that describes my type of "charm" is *politician*. I was the silent politician in school, and that is still a part of who I am today. It's not a great feeling, and I don't really think of it as positive. Have you ever felt that there is a piece of you that is a good thing, in the sense that it helps you get through each day, but when you recognize it and take ownership of it you feel uncomfortable? Well, that is how the word *politician* makes me feel. I am really too close to the word for comfort's sake. I have been told on countless occasions that I would make a great politician—and those people are right. I know I would make the best damn politician in the country. I take that back . . . most of my issues would focus on education. I would put all the other issues on hold until our education system is improved. My campaign mission would be to infuse the passion of teaching back into our schools. To allow teachers to do what they are good at. To de-emphasize large classrooms, paperwork, and red tape. Education should enrich and expand the mind; somehow we have lost that focus.

As I traveled through the education system as a true politician, I never missed a cue. I was always on time and made sure the teacher noticed I was attending to her lessons. My face was pleasant, and my eyes were always fixed on the chalkboard in front of me. I could never let my teacher find out that most of the information she was sending got lost in my brain. I learned early on that it was important that I be out of the classroom during certain times of the day. These were the times that I was the most threatened and unable to control the situation. Control had a lot to do with it. If I were able to control my daily environment to the best of my ability, I would not be caught in embarrassing situations. A lot depended on how specific teachers handled their classes. Some of them micromanaged their classrooms, which made it more difficult to slide out the back door with an excuse, while others had more loosely structured classes, which made it easier for me to escape. I also used the students in the classroom to buffer the blows. It is amazing how sitting next to an obnoxious student or a very bright student can make you blend into the wall. I was always the politician, holding a neutral platform, striving to stay in the campaign (grade) and hoping to run off with the victory at the end (moving to the next grade).

My primary goal as a politician was to create a safe place, an environment that would not expose my true self to the public. I took everything into account. All those minute details came into play: controlling where I sat in the classroom, who I sat by, the daily schedule, and even picking the right teachers, if possible. Managing to get out of class just exactly when I wanted to became my largest campaign challenge. I needed a distraction—something legitimate disguised as a good deed that would take me away from the fire . . . something like becoming a messenger boy. Upon entering every new school I attended, I would quickly seek out a safe place where I could be of help. In middle school it was the Guidance Counselor's office. In high school I used the Athletic Office in the gym. Because I was very helpful and likable to the staff who governed these offices, I was often asked to run errands during the day. I found early on that I could orchestrate when I wanted to run these errands, getting me out of situations that might have placed me in jeopardy of having to read or spell in front of my classmates. Often the things I wanted to get out of were activities that were considered fun by most of my classmates—learning games, field trips, and pep rallies. These were all situations over which I had no control and no backup plan if I should be put on the spot. Strangely enough, in some of these cases, there would be no opportunity for me to be "caught" or put on the spot, but just the thought of not being able to control the situation scared me. Control was a primary survival skill (charm).

Whereas playing the Politician worked well for me, other creative learners have learned to survive using different kinds of charms. One charm that I often see used in my adult group members is when an individual becomes educated enough about disabilities and civil rights to confront every situation with a warrior-like attitude. These "charming warriors" at first come across as being very proactive, using all their weapons to get what they want. The phrase, "knowledge is power," is the Warrior's motto. Using a sharp tongue, warriors can, in many cases, control their destinies by spouting off enough facts and definitions to immediately disarm their opponents. The Warrior's goal is to seize the moment and take no prisoners: "This is my disability. This is what I need. Give it to me." In many cases, this works very well. However, it may eventually put off the teacher as well as other individuals with learning disabilities. In many cases, Warriors find themselves on the battlefield alone, fighting their battles with little or no support from others.

Another frequently used charm is that of the Mime. Quiet, shy, and invisible, this charmer plays off the audience. He or she can mimic any situation. The Mime never lets anyone know what he or she is thinking. The face is expressionless and reflects what the teacher wants to see. This charmer goes through life never causing trouble and expects nothing in return. The Mime is the person in your class to whom you wonder if you are getting through. Although these students usually have the potential to do a lot more, they are usually so afraid of taking risks that they are content to "just get by." They do that by watching and imitating those around them, never thinking for themselves and never forming or following their own dreams. Be careful of the charming Mimes, for they will slip through the cracks.

Another charmer is the Giver, or Philanthropist. When I think of the Philanthropist, I imagine a little boy or girl setting an apple on the teacher's desk. Their motto is "To give is to receive." This charm is developed at an early age and could come from models in their home environment: "Clean your room and you can watch TV." Observing how well this works in the home environment, Philanthropists learn to apply this philosophy to a higher level. A method of manipulation. A charm disguised as an apple. These charmers are usually liked by their friends because of what they bring to the playground. Gifts in hand, they are immediately accepted into the crowd. The philanthropist also bears the gift of compliments, feeling that just a few positive words—"You look nice today" or "That was a great class"— might make a positive difference in a grade. Never negative in front of teachers, they often build the teacher up with positive feedback: "I can't believe I passed this class! I owe it all to you."

One of the most complex charmers is the Magician. This person adeptly uses smoke and mirrors to distract his or her audience (listener) long enough to vanish from the situation or to retrieve the requested information. A common characteristic of the Magician is the art of deflecting the question back to the audience in order to receive the answer. For example, if asked, "What did you think of the movie, 'Shakespeare in Love,'" the magician might not be able to quickly connect the movie title with the actual movie. In order not to appear stupid in front of his or her friends, the Magician buys time by deflecting the question back: "I haven't made my mind up yet. What did you think?" Based on the answer given by the listener, the magician is able to piece together enough information to know whether or not he or she had seen the movie. This skill is not an easy skill to develop and usually takes someone who is gifted in the art of communication to pull it off smoothly. Magicians seldom get off stage and only allow people to see exactly what they want them to see.

I have become aware of my personal survival strategies as well as the strategies of those around me. These strategies (charms) have taken me places in my life where I would not have been able to go. I do know that I succeeded in college because of lots of studying and hard work, but my ability to be a good politician played just as strong a role. Since leaving school, I have learned to acknowledge and honor my personal survival skills, keeping them close to me and in check, using them in a proactive manner rather than as a victim. The Politician gives me the gifts of flexibility and diversity that I use in my everyday life. However,

I wish my teachers and parents had been more aware of my manipulations and had given me insight into the Victim that resided within a narcissistic place somewhere inside of me. I realize that my teachers and parents could not have done this without some self-esteem building. My coach had been able to reach me because of the success I had in the water. Because of that success, I *listened* to what he said, and his teachings followed me into the classroom. Perhaps I was successful in swimming because I knew what was expected of me. Diving into the water, I knew what I had to do. With school it was different. The maze of letters, numbers, and symbols pushed me to develop the persona of the Politician. Teachers and parents need to be aware of these personas, and, when the time is right, the students need to be confronted about the manipulative strategies they use. This should be done in a unique and creative way that builds on the strengths of the charms, yet makes the student aware of the dangers that come with relying on those charms too much. Relying too heavily on charms will make it difficult for the person to grow into a mature, responsible adult.

Tips for Teachers

A Needs Statement

Help your student develop a "needs" statement. It is important that students are aware of what it takes for them to survive in the classroom, but also how to communicate what they need. Very seldom do I work with students who have this characteristic. If students were trained to say what they need in the learning process, there would be a lot less manipulation going on. By implementing this philosophy into a classroom, it would help students feel more comfortable about their own individual learning process. An example of a needs statement is:

> MARK: "Why are you still in the classroom? Let's go to the gym."
> LUKE: "I can't go right now. I need to finish up a lesson. I'll go with you tomorrow."

Students with learning disabilities who can articulate what they need in an effective way can be proactive in situations rather than manipulative. In many cases, students with learning disabilities feel the need to please everyone, not wanting to let anyone down, instead of taking care of their own personal needs. For acceptance by their peers, they will put their academic work in jeopardy. This is common for all students, but with students with learning disabilities, it is imperative that they learn to prioritize and articulate their needs. If this characteristic is not learned, it can cause failure throughout their lives, not only in school or work, but also in social situations.

Teachers can be very effective in helping students learn to state their needs. Rather than offer students particular accommodations, teachers should say to them, "Tell me what accommodations you need for this assignment." More than likely, this is the process that teachers of high school or college students use. However, if students have not been taught how to state their needs in earlier grades, they may resort to manipulation, demands, or "charms," rather than simply making an honest statement of needs. In order to develop this skill, students must be aware of the types of accommodations, modifications, and strategies available and helpful to them and how to make the appropriate match between class requirements and their own individual needs. They must begin to learn these skills as early as possible in their school careers.

Scaffolding Methods

Use scaffolding methods to help students feel successful while working as independently as possible. Sometimes teachers are manipulated by students without being aware that this manipulation is taking place. At other times, teachers are aware that students are using manipulative techniques but allow them to continue because "at least the student is making an effort." A student might approach a teacher for help with "this one little question": "Teacher, if you'll help me with this one little question, I think I can do the rest on my own." Teachers get very busy and may not realize that this student comes back time after time until the teacher has actually "helped" with every question of an entire assignment. Or worse, the teacher *does* realize he or she did the entire work sheet for the student and assumes that's OK because the student will not get behind and may feel good about completing the assignment. The reality is that doing the assignment for the student just reinforces in the student's mind that he or she cannot do the work independently.

The use of scaffolding techniques in cases like these will help the student learn to work more independently. The teacher can *guide* the student through an assignment without doing the assignment for the student. With each step the student completes on his or her own, the teacher needs to state that fact: "OK, you have completed the first step all by yourself. Tell me what you think you do next." Students who really lack self-confidence may continue to check in with the teacher even though they are working independently: "Did I do this one right? Did I do this one right?" Challenge this student to increase independent work time with something like, "I believe you could do three problems all on your own before coming to check with me. Try that." In addition to building these students' abilities to work independently, teachers may need to directly address the "charm" the students are attempting to use. Sometimes, coming up to a teacher over and over for help is also a way of demonstrating to the teacher how hard you are working. The teacher may need to directly address this by saying, "You don't need to keep showing me your paper to let me know how hard you are working. I can tell how hard you are trying when I see you sitting in your desk and when I get your papers."

Dealing with Negative "Charms"

Deal quickly and directly with students who use negative "charms" to get their way; they need more direct intervention than those who use positive charms. Teachers enjoyed having me in their classes because I worked hard at being a "good politician." Being nice and well-mannered were some of the few things I had going for me in the classroom. I have known students, however, who used negative charms to get their way. Rather than going up to a teacher and smiling cutely and saying, "If you could just get me started on this, I'm sure I can do it myself," these students either demand help or whine something like, "I can't do this. I'm lost." Not only do I hear this from adults in my LD group, but I also remember being exposed to it in the swimming pool. Swimmers would constantly say, "I can't do that set. There is no way I can make that interval." The word *can't* became a very powerful word, and at the beginning of my freshman year in high school, the coach banned it from the pool. Never could a swimmer say the word *can't*, or the set would be repeated for the whole group. This intervention on the coach's part made all the swimmers aware of the number of times *can't* was being used; needless to say, for the next year we repeated lots of sets. This lesson has stuck with me, and I have incorporated it into my personality. During the three years I was in high school, I never said the word *can't*. I think it is appropriate to ban certain negative words such as this one from the classroom. Place them up on the board or on the wall, and train the students to only use positive words. Also put up neutral words that can be used in place of the negative ones to express their feelings. Keep in mind that these words should not be too hard to read.

Direct behavioral intervention may be necessary for students who rely on negative charms. Address the behavior with the student, along with the fact that a negative attitude can be more detrimental to them than a positive one. Help the student set a reasonable goal for stopping the behavior. For instance, you might challenge the student to go fifteen minutes without saying, "I can't." Successfully completing the goal will bring you, the teacher, to the student's desk to check his or her progress. Gradually increase the time until the student is going an entire period/morning/day without saying "I can't." Success in meeting the long-term goal should be rewarded with something the student really wants to work for.

Providing Students with a Sense of Control

Give your students as many opportunities as possible to feel in control. Giving them a sense of control is one of the most important gifts you can ever give them. Students with learning disabilities do not like to be surprised. Field trips, in particular, can be very frightening. One of my biggest fears was being left behind, because I had such difficulty telling time and reading bus numbers. This meant I had to put my trust into other students in order to be sure I got to the right bus at the right time. Trust became a big issue with me; to confide my fears in someone else was unthinkable because they would know I was stupid. It would have been helpful if there had been more communication about the field trip beforehand. Teachers often told us to report to a certain building if we got lost. However, hearing this information without seeing the building was not at all helpful to me. If this information had been given again upon arrival and the building pointed out to us, some of my anxiety would have been relieved. If the buses had somehow been color-coded, that would have been helpful. My teacher and I could have easily worked this out without anyone else knowing it by placing a small colored dot on the door of my bus. As for telling time, there are now watches that talk. All of these things would have put me back in control of the situation.

Research indicates that the condition of learned helplessness is created from a traumatic event or a series of experiences in which students feel totally powerless (Jenson 1998). Depending on their age and the circumstances surrounding these experiences, students develop an unmotivated "I don't care" attitude or a helpless "I can't" attitude about life and particularly about school. In their study of the characteristics of highly successful adults with learning disabilities, Gerber and Ginsberg (1990) found that the driving factor underlying success for all of their participants was the quest to gain control of one's life. Successful adults with learning disabilities are able to take control of their lives, and the greater the degree of control, the greater the likelihood of success. Control to the adults in this study meant "making conscious decisions to take charge of one's life, and adapting and shaping oneself in order to move ahead . . . This control was the fuel that fired their success" (6).

Parents and teachers often have the best intentions when they jump in and do things for students with learning disabilities; however, helping students avoid the hard things in life does not teach them how to control those situations. Rather than removing a student from a difficult class to one that is easier or to a resource room, the teachers, student, and parents need to try every possible means of helping that student gain control of the situation without having to "quit" the class. Sometimes this is not possible, but I think teachers and parents too often take an action that removes a student from a difficult situation rather than helping him or her learn how to handle the situation in a positive manner. Students who learn positive ways to stay in control will not have to resort to manipulation and use of charms, and they will have a much better chance for success as adults.

Student Misinterpretation

Don't assume the obvious when dealing with students with learning disabilities. It is better to be too thorough than not thorough enough. Sometimes, the most common-sense classroom activities will be misunderstood by students who perceive things differently from their peers. A good example of this is misinterpreting the meaning of certain words. Students with learning disabilities often consider only one meaning of a word or make literal interpretations of words. The first time that Rosemary offered to make a standing appointment to meet with me, I took the word *standing* literally. I found it curious that she would not want to sit down to work with me but thought that maybe it was some new LD technique she was trying out. It wouldn't have been the first time I had been used as a guinea pig.

We laugh about this now because it seems so crazy that something so obvious could be misinterpreted. However, something to keep in mind when offering instruction in the classroom, whether academic or directional, is that clear and precise information is getting to the students with learning disabilities. In working with students and adults with learning disabilities, I have noticed what I call the "nodding the head syndrome." This syndrome is one that everyone uses from time to time in their lives, but for students with learning disabilities, this is a common characteristic. There is a tendency not to want to admit to the teacher or the rest of the class that we don't understand. The other side of this is when students nod their heads, truly believing they understand. The best way to get information across to these students is by using multisensory learning. Give directions in both auditory and visual manners. The most common problems that I hear about are in the area of homework. Students with learning disabilities seem to have difficulty with the instructional aspects of their homework assignments: getting the due dates correct or the instructions or even getting home with assignments. One of the most effective tools in helping to solve this problem is to post assignments on the Internet. A phone-in Homework Hotline is also very effective. To clarify instructional assignments, it is helpful if there is a single place where all important information is posted. Students also need help in learning how to organize their own personal materials. One single notebook with subject dividers works best for most students. This provides a data base of information that parents, students, and teachers can quickly draw upon. In the early grades, teachers might consider giving this notebook a personality by giving it a name. Students may even vote on the name as a class. If the notebook is viewed as a personal friend, students are less likely to lose it. The notebook should contain a pencil bag where students can keep pencils, pencil grips, sticky notes, paper clip markers, and highlighters. Throughout the day, teachers can have students highlight homework assignments and due dates in appropriate color codes. All classwork will be placed in this book, along with other important school information. Students may be required to take the notebook home each evening for parents to review the day's work and sign off. A correspondence section may be included so that parents and teachers can communicate when needed.

Overpreparation

Help your students learn to anticipate situations and *overprepare* for them. In order not to be caught in embarrassing situations, I have found myself overpreparing for most things I do. When I talk about overpreparing, I am not just spending extra time going over material, but also an exorbitant amount of energy sizing up the situation that is about to occur. For example, when traveling to another city to give a presentation, not only do I overprepare the material I will present, but I also overprepare about getting to the conference itself: How will I read the signs to get me from the airport to the hotel? How will I remember the name of my contact or the organization to which I am speaking?

Overpreparing has been one of the key factors of my success; however, with success there is always a downside. Overpreparation can be emotionally draining. Teachers need to take into account in classroom situations that students with learning disabilities need to spend more time preparing for almost everything they do. Teachers can help by offering preparation strategies, while, at the same time, helping students realize that it is sometimes OK to fly by the seat of your pants.

Works Cited

Gerber, P. J., and R. J. Ginsberg. 1990. "Identifying Alterable Patterns of Success in Highly Successful Adults with Learning Disabilities." Executive summary, United States Department of Education, Office of Special Education and Rehabilitative Services, National Institute for Disability and Rehabilitation Research, Grant #H133G80500.

Jensen, E. 1998. *Teaching with the Brain in Mind.* Alexandria, VA: Association for Supervision and Curriculum Development (ASCD).

Seven

Building a Successful Student Advocate

Another Wednesday-night-pizza writing session . . . Rosemary removed her glasses and rubbed her eyes as she repeated to me, "It's OK to use the word *disability* here." This was a statement that I had heard many times from Rosemary during the time we were writing *Faking It* together. I had chosen not to use the word *disability* anywhere in the text of *Faking It*, a deliberate choice from a confused little boy—a boy who had been labeled "disabled" from the beginning of school. Pacing, I flashed back to the second grade, where I was first initiated to the term *disabled*. The feelings of sadness, anger, and confusion rushed through me as I confronted Rosemary one more time. I would not believe I was disabled in any way. I had made it my quest to redefine the term *learning disabilities* into *creative learning abilities*, and I was not going to give in now. As I pretended to listen to Rosemary's rebuttal, images and feelings of people who used wheelchairs, of people who were blind or who had other visible disabilities ran through my head. Rosemary was talking, but I didn't hear her. These feelings drained me as Rosemary's voice filtered in. "Keep in mind, Christopher, that the word *disability* gives you rights that are helping you to succeed." It has taken several years for that statement to settle in and to understand and truly accept that I am an individual with a disability. As I pace now, watching Rosemary type, feelings of that little boy in the second grade still rush back. I am aware that no matter how much I have learned and implemented advocacy in my life, a piece of me will always fight the word *disabled*—a word that has given me so many reasonable accommodations through the law. This word has allowed me extra time on

106

tests, special adaptive software, and a reader and writer on the job. Most importantly, it has introduced me to a world of people with many types of disabilities. I have become a successful advocate first by accepting my rights under the law and, second, by paying attention and learning from the people who do it best—individuals with physical disabilities who have overwhelmed and amazed me with their abilities. To Janet, Tamara, Gene, Robin, Mark, Lamar, and for all my other friends and colleagues who have touched me and taught me the skills of successful advocacy, thank you for helping to heal that little boy.

Building success is a lifelong process that should be implemented in a child's life as early as possible. In dealing with a child with learning disabilities, building success can be challenging and requires careful planning and development. When I was eight years old, I knew the difference between doing good versus doing bad; in between good and bad sat my confusion. My friends went on to third grade—which was good. I repeated the second grade—which, in my young mind, was bad. I believe my parents knew at this point in my life that school would never be easy for me. What they, as well as I, had no clue about was how this learning disability would affect all parts of my life, lurking around each corner, following me like a shadow outside the classroom door.

Somewhere between the second and fifth grades, I named my shadow after myself—Loser. Loser was bigger than I. He interfered with everything I tried to do, weighing on me like an anchor on a boat, slowing me down and making me clumsy in a sea of words. Loser became my disability. It was my way of detaching my stupidity (disability) from my core being. Loser was going to do everything he could to beat me down. I had to force Loser to take a back seat by repressing the urge to listen to the moans, groans, and put-downs when something went wrong.

As an adult I have formed my own model for repressing "the loser" in me. I call it my Self-Advocacy Building Block Model. I developed this model over a period of many years of working with individuals who struggle with self-esteem and with professionals who gave me insight into the needs of adults with learning disabilities. One of the most enlightening experiences for me was my work with the LD reasearch and Training Ceter, a collaborative effort between the University of Georgia Learning Disabilities Center and the Roosevelt Warm Springs Institute for Rehabilitation. It was there that I began laying the foundation for this model.

To begin developing the Advocate within myself, it was important for me to consider two personal components, which I visualize as building blocks: *self-empowerment* and *self-involvement*. I used the building blocks to shape success in my everyday life and to develop my internal advocate. I believe self-empowerment and self-involvement are the key components in teaching self-advocacy skills. If taught effectively, these two components complement each other (Figure 7-1).

In reflecting back on how I became a successful advocate, I looked closely at myself. What characteristics had I developed along my educational path that led me to be self-empowered? In searching for this answer, I have come up with three areas that influenced my development: knowing that I have a learning disability, understanding my disability from a personal perspective, and being able to talk comfortably about my disability (Figure 7-2).

The first area is knowing that you have a disability. At this level, the individual becomes aware that he or she has a disability, usually through some type of psychological evaluation. Unfortunately, the only person who typically understands the psychological report is the psychologist who administered the assessment. It is important for parents and teachers to find a way to understand the assessment, because the assessment is one of the keys to unlocking an individual's potential. Because this is a disability associated with school, learning disabilities are often identified with subjects such as reading, writing, and math. It is important that a good battery of tests be selected to identify the *processing* deficit in the brain that is affecting a person's *ability* to read, write, and do math. A good evaluation

Figure 7–1 *Self-Advocacy Building Block Model*

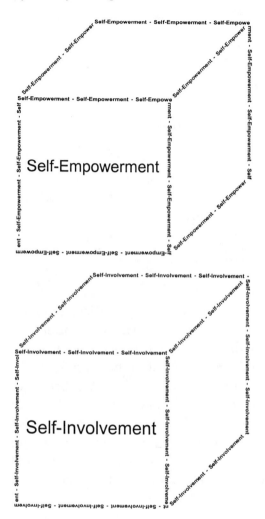

Figure 7–2 *Characteristics of the Self-Empowerment Building Block*

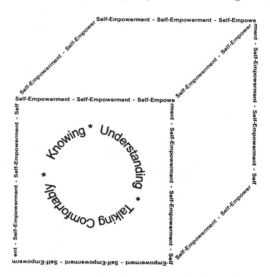

should also include tests of acuity, intellectual ability, achievement, language ability, and social and emotional status. Depending on who conducts the assessment, there is often specific terminology attached to the learning disability label, such as *dyslexia* or *cognitive processing deficit*. School evaluations are often subject-oriented and will specify deficit subject areas, such as "math disability" or "reading disability." It is important that students are exposed to the medical terms or other terminology associated with the learning disability label. Being able to communicate this terminology will be vital throughout life's transitions. For example, I know I have a cognitive processing deficit that affects my ability to accurately process written and spoken language. Specifically, I have difficulty processing auditory information, which hinders my ability to tell the difference between similar-sounding words. I also have difficulty processing visual information, which affects my ability to read or write words that look similar. Many times when driving on the interstate, I find myself searching for a Sonny's Bar-B-Q, only to find myself walking into a Shoney's. I hate that!

The second area focuses on understanding one's disability. This area is where the individual personalizes his or her disability, taking ownership and learning to express difficulties through analogies or stories. It is important that the story be vivid and powerful enough that people can easily relate to it. For example, while participating in a learning disabilities self-advocacy workshop, my brother came up with the analogy for his learning disability. Craig visualizes his disability by putting himself into a track meet. As he starts the race, he always sees himself on the outside lane, which is lined with hurdles, while everyone else runs within the inner lanes, unencumbered by any obstacles. As his opponents swiftly pass him, Craig struggles with the hurdles placed in front of him. Tripping over the hurdles, he falls and has to get up and start again, and is left behind by his opponents. This story allows Craig the opportunity to express his frustration with his disability in a manner he can understand. Stories like this help de-emphasize the frustration and anxiety that students often feel about this invisible disability.

Another analogy that I find interesting comes from a gifted adult with learning disabilities. She describes her disability as a shouting match between her left brain and her right brain, much like the Democrat and Republican parties. A third example was given to me when I was conducting a workshop for Adult Basic Education professionals. When asking the participants—who did not have learning disabilities—to give me an example of how they might visualize a learning disability, I got mixed examples. As I went around the room and listened to the participants, not one of them was able to communicate an effective descriptive analogy until we got to a woman who was hard of hearing. She described her disability, which she felt would be similar to that of a person with a learning disability, as "driving in pea soup," only getting small chunks of information while desperately trying to find her way out using her windshield wipers. Using personal stories and analogies can release the frustration, anxiety, stress, and tension that spreads so extensively in this population.

111

The third area of self-empowerment is being able to talk comfortably about one's disability. This is not as easy as it sounds. It takes practice and patience to decide the appropriate way to disclose a learning disability. I have found, in many cases, that my description changes depending on the person to whom I am disclosing. For instance, if I am talking with a family member, I am more likely to talk about the emotional issues that concern me. If I'm talking with a friend, usually I find myself making the explanation short and to the point. If disclosing to a teacher or professor, it is important that I combine the technical terminology with my own personal analogy, stressing my past accomplishments and the extra effort I plan to make in the teacher's class.

An important element I advise students to keep in mind, when communicating with others about their disabilities, is the use of humor. Humor puts people at ease and, used effectively, can make the difference in getting accommodations, making friends, or even getting and maintaining a job. I use humor on a daily basis in regard to my speech problem. Because my brain processes sounds differently, my speech is affected. Even though I was raised in the South, my speech disguises itself as that of someone from New Jersey or, sometimes, more exotic locales such as Australia or England. Last year I stopped by a bagel shop in my hometown of Jacksonville, Florida. Never reading the actual sign, but looking instead at the big fluorescent donut-shaped bagel in the window, I knew I had the right place. I found myself lying as the cashier asked me where I was from. Nervously, and keenly aware of the line of eager bagel eaters behind me, I slipped into a familiar character role. I was now a person from another place. "This time I'll make it New York," I thought. "That usually works quickest." Needless to say, I had no idea that I was standing in the New York Bagel Shop of Jacksonville, Florida—a situation that led to complicated machinations on my part trying to explain to my "fellow statesmen" where exactly in New York I was from, why I was in Jacksonville, and so forth. Go figure.

There are two aspects of disclosure that are not humorous but often surface when individuals are experimenting with disclosure techniques: victimization and narcissism. It is important that the individual with the learning disability not assume the role of Victim. This is an easy hole to fall into, and it is not uncommon for the most effective self-advocates to find themselves cautiously skirting the edge of this familiar place. Another role at which I have to work hard to avoid is that of Narcissist. I have learned by watching myself and others that narcissism is a survival characteristic that often develops from years of self-absorption in dealing with a disability. This attribute may result in individuals expecting too much help or refraining from asking for any help at all. This is also a dangerous place to be and may isolate individuals with learning disabilities from the important support systems they need to get through their daily activities.

In summary, the Self-Empowerment Building Block includes the following:

1. Knowing the terminology associated with the disability
   - Being exposed to the psychological evaluation and using the evaluation to graph out one's strengths and weaknesses
2. Understanding the disability
   - Being able to describe the disability through stories or analogies
   - Being able to list strengths as well as weaknesses
3. Talking comfortably with others about the disability
   - Articulating a well-rehearsed statement that combines the technical understanding with a visual analogy

Now moving on to the next building block—self-involvement—I have come up with three areas that influenced my development: risk, trust, and persistence (Figure 7-3).

The self-involvement building block is the second component to developing the inner self-advocate. In order to build self-advocacy skills, students must be actively involved in the decisions that affect their lives. Due to the broad spectrum of their learning disabilities, these decisions will not only involve academics, but also

Figure 7–3 *Characteristics of the Self-Involvement Building Block*

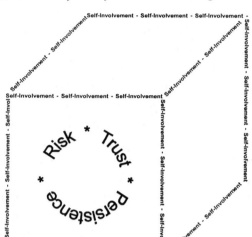

should involve career, social, and personal decisions. In many cases, parents and teachers assume they know what is best for the child and tend to drive the decision-making process, often without any input at all from the child. Some of the most positive times in my life were being involved in the decision-making process of my swimming career. Throughout my career, major decisions had to be made, such as switching teams, going to meets, dealing with coaches, and choosing a college swimming program. It was important for me to be involved and to be able to make my own decisions throughout this process, whether they turned out to be good or bad decisions in the end. This process helped prepare me to get involved with decisions I later had to make about my learning disabilities. I had always chosen to stay in the background in regard to early decisions about my learning disabilities. It wasn't until college that I was forced to face my learning disabilities head-on and take an active part in the decisions that would affect the rest of my life. My early involvement in the decision-making process for swimming helped me transition to my involvement in learning disabilities. In looking back to that time, I can clearly see how risk taking, trust, and persistence helped me develop into a confident decision-maker and self-advocate.

The first area in the development of self-involvement is risk-taking. Even though taking risks puts the student in a vulnerable, scary place, it is a crucial element of success.

Because it is often difficult for students to risk their vulnerability, I feel that this is an area that parents and teachers need to explore together. Just as students need to develop academic skills, they also need to develop risk-taking skills, and these are not skills that just automatically develop. Students with learning disabilities need lots of encouragement. Most people perceive risks to be major events, such as presenting a speech in front of a large audience, changing schools, going to college, getting married, climbing Mt. Everest, skydiving, and so on. However, there are many small risks that can help foster the ability to take larger risks, such as asking someone out on a date, deciding to swim in an event in which you do not excel, or going on field trips. Introducing risk-taking activities in small increments such as these helps prepare individuals to attempt the larger risks that challenge them over a lifetime.

One of the biggest things parents and teachers can do is to realize that students with learning disabilities take a risk simply by walking through the front door of school everyday year after year. I know this because I put myself in that vulnerable place for eighteen years. I was taking a risk just by staying, even though many times I tried to get around the system by hiding in the gym during reading class or getting sick right before spelling bees. Still, I was in the race. It is important for teachers and parents to acknowledge the huge risk students take on a daily basis. They should be commended for simply returning to that negative environment (school) day after day, while being encouraged to continue. Thinking back on it now, I feel good that I was able to stick it out for all those years. As I go through my life now as an adult, I know I am a stronger person because I took the risk of walking through those school doors every year.

Developing trust is the second area of the self-involvement building block. Students with learning disabilities often have difficulty with trust issues. This is because they have been beaten down by the education system for so many years. Teachers have the ability to change this cycle by taking time, being honest, and ensuring the student that he or she has the capability of making it in school. One of the most memorable challenges I ever had to face was learning how to disclose my learning disabilities to my college professors. To me they were gods—academicians hovering over their students. How was I supposed to confront them about my struggles in the classroom? It was obvious to me and everyone else that most professors have a passion for their field of study and have achieved high levels of learning. How could they possibly relate to a student who struggled to read and write simple words? What could I possibly say that would make my professors understand that I wasn't dumb and that I could succeed in their classrooms if given a chance to use appropriate accommodations and modifications? As I was learning the technique and process of self-disclosure with Rosemary, I realized that my biggest hurdle was not in trusting the professors but in trusting myself, because, even at this point, I didn't quite believe I wasn't dumb and that I could actually make it in their classes. I started the process by learning to trust Rosemary. I allowed myself to take the risk of self-disclosure because *she* said I wasn't dumb and that I could make it in their classes. Learning to trust Rosemary was a challenge in itself. She represented the Education System that had tried to hold me back for years. I learned to trust Rosemary through shear determination—not because I wanted to stay in college to learn, but because of athletics. Athletics was my motivation, and I knew Rosemary was my only possible link to staying involved with my passion, sports. I was smart enough to realize I had no other choices at this point in my academic career. It was time for me to either sink or swim. Maybe it was a good thing that swimming was my sport of choice.

Recognizing the motivation in your students will be a key component to gaining their trust. Tapping into that motivation is the way to make the sale. Students with problems in academics are often very involved in outside activities such as sports, photography, music, and so forth, and these activities can be the motivation that teachers use to gain the trust of their students. I feel strongly that students' motivational aspects should be listed in their Individual Education Plans (IEPs) and incorporated into the annual goals and objectives. Rosemary knew that she had an ace in the hole: swimming. It gave her the upper hand in building trust. Her goal became my goal. Everything was centered around my continuing to swim for the University of Georgia. Learning grew from that motivation. After a period of time of working with Rosemary, I began to trust her enough to listen to what she said. Through periods of professor–student role playing, I came to trust my ability to communicate effectively to my professors. The interesting thing about learning how to disclose to my professors, or anyone else, was that it wasn't so much what I said, but how I said it. I learned that using the right voice tone, eye contact, and effective analogies to describe my learning style made my ability to disclose very effective. I even began to believe my own words.

Another important factor in building trust in your students is the ability to let go. Rosemary could have taken the safe and easy way out. She could have called the professors herself and asked them to give me the modifications I was guaranteed under the law. However, that would not have taught me the lesson of self-advocacy. Rosemary taught me the skills I needed to advocate for myself, and then she trusted me to go out on my own and use them. Teachers and parents have to trust students enough to let them go.

This leads to the third and final area of self-involvement: persistence. It is imperative that students with learning disabilities develop the characteristic of persistence, because they will be faced with unique challenges throughout their lives. It is common for students with learning disabilities to spend hours and hours studying, only to end up with a barely passing score on a test. They may need to leave class every time a test is given in order to have special modifications. They may be unable to look up phone numbers in a phone book or write down directions to a friend's house. Facing unknown challenges every day takes its toll and may result in high levels of stress and anxiety as well as tendencies to leave tasks unfinished or unstarted. Teachers can help their students learn to remain optimistic while, at the same time, to be realistic. This can be accomplished by the student and teacher working together to set realistic goals. It is an important process to openly discuss what the student feels he or she wants to make on an exam, for instance. Some students may feel that if they study enough, they can make an A, while others may feel they have no chance of passing at all. Once the teacher knows how the student feels about something, he or she can help guide the student in setting a reasonable goal that is truly attainable.

Sometimes, even with good planning, reasonable goals cannot be obtained. Let's take Johnny, who has set a goal of making a B on an English test. Even though he follows the study plan, he barely passes the test. He goes home, and the first question from Mom is, "How did you do on the test?" Not only is he disappointed with himself, now he has to relate his failure to his parents and spend a night stewing and beating himself up over another failure. If Johnny had a backup plan that had been worked out between him and his teacher before the test, things could be quite different. A backup plan entails that the student and teacher come back together and analyze what went wrong—why the goal was not reached. This takes some of the pressure off of Johnny as he enters the house to tell the bad news to his mom. Instead of being totally negative, Johnny will be able to relay that he did not do well on the test but that he and his teacher are going to sit down together the next day and figure out why. This allows some breathing room for Johnny to constructively consider what went wrong and will encourage him to come up with some solutions to bring in to the teacher the next day. The student is taking ownership of the problem, while the teacher is continuously in the background being supportive and encouraging. Teachers are more likely to work with students who take ownership and responsibility, but I think it is the teacher's responsibility to help students learn how to make reasonable goals and to give them the skills to reach them.

I wish my teachers had talked to me after I failed to do well on tests or assignments. Throughout all my years of swimming, I can't remember a time when, after a bad race, I did not walk over to the coach immediately to discuss what went wrong. Even though I usually remained disappointed with my performance, these meetings gave me hope that I would do a better job the next time. I realize now that I was taught to do this by my coach, but it was always my responsibility to approach him and find out what went wrong. I wish I had been taught to actively engage my teachers after a bad performance. Instead, my teachers would hardly make eye contact with me when handing back "bad" papers. In sports activities, the coach's goal is to have each player produce at peak performance levels, usually resulting in an efficiently run team. Every player, whether on the bench or not, is expected to reflect this attitude. With this in mind, if I were a teacher, I would make sure that I knew the strengths and weaknesses of each of my students, and when one of them failed, I would be sure the backup plan was in place.

In summary, there are three areas within the self-involvement block:

1. Risk taking, which may simply involve having the courage to show up day after day
   - Make students aware of day-to-day risks and commend them for accepting these challenges.
   - Prepare and plan for future risks that will need to be taken.

- Intertwine small risks with large risks, remembering that not every risk has to be something large.
- Include risk-taking skills in IEP goals.
2. Trust: helping students learn to trust by tapping into their motivation while, at the same time, trusting that the students can handle things on their own
   - Give trust time to develop.
   - Make personal connections to the students by relaying things that are difficult for you.
   - Be honest but positive with students about their disabilities.
3. Persistence: helping students maintain their optimism while being realistic and reaching for success one goal at a time
   - Start off by setting small and realistic goals.
   - Always having a backup plan to ensure development of ownership and future success.

Teacher Tips

Development Through Analogies

Help your students develop an analogy for their learning process. In this important life-long exercise, the teacher should consider guiding students by first providing examples of analogies. After discussing analogies and giving students time to think about their own, have the students use some type of expressive technique to illustrate their personal analogies. For example, one of my analogies involves the visualization of several islands throughout my brain. Bridges connect the islands. The information I need to retrieve determines the island I need to visit. If I were asked for the name of the restaurant where I ate the night before, I picture myself getting in my car and driving to the appropriate island. It never fails that when I get up to the bridge that leads to that island, I encounter a flashing billboard that says, "Under construction!" Frustrated, but determined, I head to another bridge. This bridge has a sign warning—"Icy conditions. Drive slowly." So I pull my car over to the side and put chains on my tires and then proceed slowly across the bridge to retrieve the name of the restaurant. This analogy gives me an outlet to visualize my learning process.

Even though the analogy does not cover the full range of my disability, it does give me a descriptive outlet to provide to others who need to understand. When Rosemary first taught me to express my learning disability through a story or analogy, I remember feeling a great relief, as if a weight had fallen from my shoulders. For the first time, I had a way to express the complicated process that was going on in my brain. It is important, when doing this exercise, that teachers give guidance to the students on a particular area of difficulty they would like to express. In my example, I used the word *retrieval*. Different analogies work better for other processing problems I have. Students can begin the process of creating an analogy in a variety of ways, including dramatic interpretation, drawing or painting, oral or written descriptions, stories, sculpture, and so on. Eventually, students do need to be able to clearly and vividly articulate the analogy to others.

Development Through Role Play

Help your students learn to talk about their strengths and weakness through role play. For years and years, students with learning disabilities struggle with academics, often focusing on the remediation of basic skills such as reading and spelling. By the time they graduate from high school, they are keenly aware of all the things they cannot do. When they go to interview for their first job, however, the first question often asked is, "Tell me about your strengths—why should I hire you for this job?" The first thing that may be articulated is something like, "I'm OK in math and pretty good in science." They relate their strengths to course work they may have struggled with the least instead of providing the interviewer with positive character traits they possess, such as persistence, creativity, the ability to "think outside the box," or the willingness to take risks and achieve goals, and so forth. We are doing our students a disservice by not teaching them to capitalize on and promote these positive attributes. One of the best techniques for accomplishing this is to have students role play instances in which they discuss their strengths and their ability to manage their weaknesses.

One of the role-playing scenarios I use with young children is to tell them that a cartoon hero, such as Superman or Wonder Woman, is coming to visit the class. I ask the students to tell me the good things they will say about themselves, making sure they are stressing the positive things they can do. This exercise may start with make-believe powers the students possess, but eventually, with the teacher's guidance, students will truly think about their strengths. It takes time to whittle down the imaginative stories, but eventually you can come up with a list of characteristics that each student can proudly hand over to Superman or Wonder Woman. An exercise such as this is a way to start the process of recognizing positive characteristics that could last a lifetime. This exercise works well with all ages just by changing the scenarios.

Development of Leadership Skills

Help build leadership skills by assigning classroom responsibilities. One of the most effective ways of building self-esteem is to provide opportunities for students to learn and practice leadership skills. One of the best leadership assignments is one in which the student with the learning disability gets to play the role of Expert. For instance, nine-year-old Diane may be placed in charge of the computer stations in the classroom. Her job might be to supervise the cleanup and the turning on and off of systems. Ideally, she reports to the teacher and the teacher gives her important information to relay to her classmates, such as information about new software programs. Placing those who are struggling academically in long-term leadership positions can build self-esteem and open communication paths between teachers and students.

Development of Student Confidence

Help students gain confidence by providing them with opportunities to experience success. Many students with learning difficulties fail to put forth effort in the classroom because they are afraid to risk the possibility of failure. Teachers can take steps to break this cycle of failure in the classroom by giving the students work and materials they are capable of completing successfully. By gradually increasing the difficulty of the material, teachers can help these students gain a true sense of accomplishment. Planning ahead to help these students make contributions to classroom discussions or activities will also give them a taste of success. For instance, you might tell these students that you are planning to ask them to do math problems on the board the next day. Specify the problems and encourage them to practice the problem at home the night before, perhaps even demonstrating the problem to their parents. This will help them to be successful in front of their peers. Similarly, you might tell these students that you will be asking them certain questions during class discussion the next day, giving them time to research the questions and compose their answers. Successful experiences such as these will encourage the students to become more confident and take more risks. Success builds success.

Success Through Outside Activities

Help students find activities outside of school in which they can be successful. While traveling around the country and speaking to groups about the development of self-advocacy skills, this is the one area I stress above all others. Students need continuing positive interactions throughout their lives. School may not be the best place for this to happen, particularly in the beginning. Teachers need to communicate this to parents and help them understand the importance of outside activities. I cannot tell you the number of times I have heard, "Should I pull my child out of soccer because his or her grades are suffering?" Usually I stop breathing. My immediate concern is that they have even considered this—that this parent does not realize that soccer may be the only positive thing in this child's life. I contribute my success throughout school to an outside activity: swimming. I have very few positive memories of school prior to the fifth grade, when I started swimming competitively. When I started swimming, people in school started recognizing me. It didn't matter so much whether or not I was great at this activity. What mattered was that I was doing it.

Development of Self-Esteem

Build self-esteem by personalizing your lessons whenever possible. Find ways to incorporate students' names and interests into your lessons and assignments. Simply using a student's name in a math problem or story can spark his or her interest. If the student has a paper route, create math problems requiring students to calculate how much a child earns delivering papers under various conditions. For students who collect Beanie Babies, Pokemon cards, coins, and so on, create story problems that use the children's names and involve the buying, selling, and trading of these items. Seeing their names in print makes children feel important. There are specialized educational software programs that allow teachers or students to personalize lessons by adding names or specific student interests. There are also multimedia interactive CDs now available that allow students to become active participants in learning. These are nonthreatening to students with learning disabilities and often have features built in to immediately reward success.

Development of Student Investment

Find ways to help your students become invested in their own learning process. Involve your students in their own education. Have your students grade their own tests and assignments. This may increase their investment in their schoolwork. Work with the students to create a method to chart their progress. Teaching this type of responsibility offers the students a better picture of what they are learning. I remember, in high school, that the English class in which I was most involved was one in which we had to read and evaluate each others' papers as a whole class. We were given a rubric at the beginning of the year, which we used each week to evaluate the paper of another student in the class. In using this method, it is important that the teacher work with the student with learning disabilities to make sure that the student has support in editing the paper before the class reads it. This is a wonderful way to make the student aware of the criteria as well as the audience to whom he or she is writing.

Development of a Sense of Humor

Help your students develop a sense of humor. Developing a sense of humor about learning disabilities gives students a tool for meeting all of the challenges they will have to face as they grow up. People with physical disabilities are often very successful in using humor to make others around them feel more comfortable. It's even more important for people with hidden disabilities to feel comfortable enough with themselves to laugh at their own mistakes. This helps them to not take themselves and life so seriously and to put their disabilities in an entirely different perspective. I think one of the best ways to encourage students to lighten up about their mistakes is for teachers to allow students to see them making mistakes. If teachers are comfortable with their own mistakes and willing to joke about them, students will feel more relaxed about their own mistakes.

Mentoring Programs

Help students get involved in mentoring programs. In many cases in which I have been working with students, I have found that teachers and parents are often too close to the student to offer objective support. An outside mentor can do this. Mentoring programs for students with learning disabilities can take different avenues. One type of mentor may be someone the student can relate to who does not have learning disabilities but shares the same interests and can act as a sounding board for both academic and social activities. This may be someone from a nearby university tutoring program or sports program or a family friend. It needs to be someone with whom the student is comfortable and to whom he or she can relate. Although this mentor may not be an expert on learning disabilities, he or she needs to be aware of and empathetic to the challenges presented by the disability.

Another type of mentor is a person who has learning disabilities. This mentor should be someone who is dealing positively with his or her learning disabilities and is a strong self-advocate. Good places to find such a mentor might be local advocacy groups and college or high school learning disabilities programs.

A third type of mentoring would be for the students themselves to become mentors to younger individuals with learning disabilities. The teacher may need to work with the young student-mentor until he or she develops the skills needed to become a positive influence in the life of another child. At times, this type of mentoring will bring up issues for the student-mentor that will spur his or her own growth and development as a self-advocate. A wish of mine would be to see strong student-advocates become involved in the development of educational programs or IEPs for younger students with learning disabilities.

Interdisability Match-ups

Match students with learning disabilities with students who have other disabilities. Matching students with learning disabilities with other students or individuals with physical disabilities can offer a unique spin on developing self-advocacy skills. Earlier in this chapter, we talked about narcissism and how individuals with learning disabilities use narcissism as a tool to get through their everyday lives. In working with other people with disabilities, I have found myself de-emphasizing my own disability while, at the same time, emphasizing my strengths. For example, I often collaborate with an attorney-friend of mine who happens to be blind. Tamara has a memory like an elephant. She can retain any facts or figures she hears and can spell any word in the dictionary correctly. This helps me because I rely on her for those things, both in meetings and in social situations. Tamara can rely on me for my strong nonverbal skills. When we work together, she can be the voice and the memory, while I can be the eyes, picking up the body language and other nonverbal reactions of the people around us. She also relies on me for my ability to describe in detail things around her (e.g., her dog). Tamara has told me on many occasions that I am her best source of visual descriptions. We make a great team.

Matching up people with disabilities with each other can also teach creative problem solving. Over the last several years, I have had the opportunity to work with people who have all types of disabilities, and I often find myself using techniques and strategies that I have learned from my colleagues with physical disabilities. These individuals go through each day developing creative independent-living skills in order to survive and prosper. Some of the independent-living strategies include assistive technology solutions, such as talking clocks and voice organizers, which can also be very helpful to individuals with learning disabilities. Look around for opportunities that provide your students with the possibilities of developing such relationships.

Long-Term Class Projects

Involve your students in a long-term class project. A long-term project can incorporate all of the characteristics involved in building self-advocacy abilities. In particular, a long-term project helps students learn persistence as well as organizational and leadership skills. Ideally, the project should include an outcome that is a physical product or will have a long-lasting effect. One of the most positive memories I have of my early-childhood education is working on a long-term project. In my case, it happened to be a small wooden stool that had a secret compartment, which I made during the second grade. I realize now that this project gave me a taste of many characteristics that I have today.

First, I was able to take ownership of the stool, which gave the project value to me. I looked forward to working on it every day over the nine-month school year. The stool also gave me patience. It was a slow and detailed process in which I made mistakes along the way. I learned that mistakes were not the end of the world; there was always a way to fix them. Another positive thing about the project, in my mind at that time, was that this had nothing to do with academics. I got to use my hands and creativity. I know now that academics were heavily involved. I had to learn prediction and estimation skills, measurement, design techniques, and overall problem-solving skills. The teacher did not give us a preconceived design. We had choices about how we wanted to construct our stool, and I knew that I wanted something with a secret compartment so I could hide things from my sister and brother (and in later years, lots of good teenage-boy stuff).

There are many activities teachers can choose for long-term projects (and they don't even have to involve secret compartments). A long-term community service project is a great way to involve the entire class while, at the same time, encouraging individual ownership and success. For example, the class might choose to host a year's worth of community blood drives. Of course, the project would involve academic learning, such as learning about blood, the circulatory system, and so forth, but, more importantly, it would create opportunities for students to make long- and short-term goals and to develop the persistence to follow through with them. Students would also have the opportunity to take on roles that require risk taking. For example, they will have to contact community leaders and work with a variety of public agencies in order to be successful. They will learn to assess their progress and their failures and that they will make and survive making mistakes. If the entire class is involved from the beginning, they will learn the concept of interdependence, along with the responsibilities that come from collaborating with others.

Eight

Tech Me: Assistive Technology Tips

*A*ssistive technology (AT) can open a world of success to individuals with learning disabilities. This chapter will introduce you to the vast opportunities that lie within the field of AT. For, school systems have placed emphasis on the remediation of basic classroom skills. There are thousands of educational software programs that are designed specifically to focus on remediation. This chapter is not about remediation, but about accommodation and modification. I will be reviewing the adaptive software and equipment that can help level the playing field for students with learning disabilities. My intention throughout this chapter is to share with you the top AT strategies that are working with students throughout the country. I will be drawing from my personal use of AT as well as from leading AT specialists. Please keep in mind as you go through this chapter that, just as different learning strategies work for individual learners, AT is also individualized. A piece that works effectively with one student may not work at all for another. Another important fact to keep in mind is that the most expensive AT is not always the best.

The emphasis on AT includes all disabilities. AT is not just for people with learning disabilities. In fact, historically, the field of AT started with the sensory and physical disability areas. The recent discovery of the value of AT has actually brought people with learning disabilities closer to people with physical and sensory disabilities. AT has begun to help in the development of a stronger, more unified voice for the national learning disabilities movement. In the past, when referring to this hidden disability, there was an emphasis on trying to comprehend the intricacies of the disability itself. AT has brought a fresh focus to the field. Instead of trying to "fix" the learning disability, now there is an emphasis on leveling the playing field. Teachers, advocates, parents, and students now have something substantial and tangible to talk about—AT.

What AT works?

It is difficult learn?

What type of technical support is offered?

How can I afford it?

Questions such as these have helped the field look closely at technological accommodations. People with disabilities are working together more closely to share resources and experiences with products. We are becoming stronger advocates with AT, which is leading to the potential development of a much-needed national network of AT consumer reports. I think people with disabilities may have benefited more than any other group from the explosion of technological advances over the past decade. AT provides individuals with disabilities more independence and productivity than ever before.

As a consumer, I can speak from experience that technology plays an extremely important part in my life. Without it, I would not be able to hold the job I have now. Through matching up the appropriate technology with my specific disability, I have been able to compensate for my processing deficits. Throughout my day, I have put into place adaptive software and equipment that allows me the freedom to be more independent and productive. I start my day off with a talking alarm clock that speaks the accurate time so I will not misread it. Due to my inability to read and comprehend newspapers and magazines, I rely on the National Public Radio and local news stations to keep up with current news and information. I keep up with the latest best-sellers by listening to them on tape. I organize my day with an electronic organizer that connects to my laptop computer. At work, I use a computer screen reader as well as software that will allow me to translate text to speech. For writing, I use a talking word processor with word-prediction/abbreviation software. I also use a Franklin Speaking Dictionary that offers portability for me throughout the day. It has taken years of trial and error for me to find the exact technology that works best for me. In addition, I have had to make sure that the different types of software work together on my computer without conflicting. Technology provides me with a means to communicate more effectively. It does not "fix" my learning disabilities, nor does it provide complete accuracy.

I could try to explain the impact that AT has had on the lives of individuals with disabilities, but Carmela Cunningham and Norman Coombs state it perfectly in their book, *Information Access and Adaptive Technology* (1997):

> There are 48 million people with disabilities in the United States. Their disabilities range from limited mobility because of things like heart attacks, sports injuries, and missing limbs, to people who can't quite hear what you're saying because they heard too much gunfire in Vietnam. There are people who have been blind since birth, and people who lost some of all of their sight later in life. People with speech problems, people with dyslexia and people whose feet just won't do what their brains tell them to do. There are all kinds of disabilities, and we all are subject to acquiring any one of those disabilities on any given day.
>
> Forty-eight million people is getting awfully close to 20 percent of the total American population. That's almost one in every five people, and no matter how you slice it, that's a lot of people to tell they can't have their piece of the American pie.
>
> In 1990, the United States spent more than $120 billion through a variety of federal, state, and private support payment structures to assist people with disabilities. Those payments came in the form of Social Security Disability Income, Food Stamps, Medicaid, Medicare, Workmen's Compensation, insurance company payments, and direct payments from businesses. We spent another $3 billion that year in rehabilitation programs.

> We spend billions of dollars to support people with disabilities. But the fact is that while we pay many of those people to sit at home, a large number of them can earn their own livelihoods. One-half of the people with disabilities in the United State are between the ages of 16 and 64—working age. Seventy-one percent of people with disabilities are unemployed. . . . That's too many people to deny the right to earn their own living. (xv–v)

With these facts in mind, what, exactly, is AT?

AT is an important piece of the support system individuals with learning disabilities require to achieve success. AT is any item, piece of equipment, or product that is used to increase, maintain, or improve the abilities of individuals with disabilities—tools to promote independence across all areas of daily living. These common tools extend from low-tech, low-cost items to high-tech, more expensive devices. Low-tech devices require little or no training; high-tech devices may require extensive training.

Technology can affect the lives of people with learning disabilities in daily living, whether it's in the classroom, at work, in the home, or in other social settings. The simplicity and ready availability of low-tech devices should not be overlooked. Inexpensive color highlighters, for example, can help students with reading difficulties distinguish between words that appear the same, like *proud, pound,* and *pond.* Teachers and parents can help the student highlight the troublesome words in different colors and make the reader visually aware of the differences between these words. Such training leads the student to a higher level of awareness of his or her disabilities. High-tech devices, such as an optical character-recognition (OCR) system, provides a means of entering text or printed material directly into a computer by use of a scanner. Once the text has been scanned into the computer, it can be read back to the user by means of a speech synthesizer. Another useful accommodation is a speech-recognition system that operates in conjunction with specially equipped personal computers. Such programs enable the user to dictate to the computer, converting oral language to written text.

New technological systems and their applications continue to evolve rapidly. In the recent past, technologies now applied to individuals with learning disabilities were originally developed for people with other disabilities. OCR programs, to select one example, appeared at first for individuals with visual impairments or blindness. Only recently were these programs found to be effective in the learning disability community.

Technology, in itself, is not the answer to all problems faced by people with learning disabilities. Technology does, however, provide valuable accommodations that allow students to participate in the regular classroom with everyone else. Those seeking technological assistance should focus not on the device, but on what the device can do for the individual in need. The fit must be right. The biggest or most expensive device may not always be the best fit. The key to selecting the most appropriate tool involves many elements: seeking a thorough team evaluation, finding the resources to obtain the technology, customizing the technology to make the best fit, and providing the time, as well as the patience, for training.

Reading Difficulties

Problem: Individuals with learning disabilities may have difficulty with understanding what they read. This difficulty stems from an inability to decode and/or comprehend written information due to an information-processing deficit. This deficit may be visual and/or auditory.

Some of the most effective devices for individuals with reading disabilities take a multisensory approach. This approach uses other sensory modes, such as hearing and sight, to assist students who have visual and/or auditory processing deficits. Individuals with learning disabilities may have difficulty processing visual information, perceiving words incorrectly. They may often look up while reading and lose their place. They may also have difficulty recognizing their own written mistakes. ATs can make visual tasks less complicated and less strenuous.

There are reading aids that will do the following:

- Enter a text into a computer through a scanner
- Read back a text, scanned in or typewritten, as the words are highlighted on the screen
- Provide access to printed materials through tapes, CD-ROMs, and special Internet services
- Magnify text and graphics
- Alter colors, font, or print size
- Provide materials through videotape or videodisk
- Provide an electronic scanning reading pen

Reading Difficulties Strategies

Books on Tape and Computer Disks: There are two different services to utilize for books on tape and disks. Recording for the Blind and Dyslexic (RFB&D) is a nonprofit service organization providing academic and professional books on audiocassette. This service requires a registration fee and yearly membership service charge. School systems, colleges, and universities can purchase institutional memberships. RFB&D has materials in all subject areas, from grade four to the postgraduate level. RFB&D notes that more than half of the people who use RFB&D's services have a learning disability—not a visual disability. An RFB&D application requires a signature by a professional in either medicine or psychology.

Although best known for their academic and professional books on audiotape, RFB&D also sells a computer disk collection called Electronic Text (E-Text). This collection consists largely of reference materials (e.g., computer manuals, reference works, specialized dictionaries, law books, a thesaurus, and the Bible), which can be used on an individual's personal computer and works with a screen reader, a software program that reads text aloud. The E-Text on floppy disk is available for both IBM-compatible PC or Macintosh systems. Because most of the computer disks and audiotapes are reference materials, RFB&D's search and retrieval software program, BookManager, is especially useful. Audiotaped books need special-playback four-track recorders (explained below). E-Text can be used with your personal computer with a screen reader and speech synthesizer equipment.

The National Library Service for the Blind and Physically Handicapped (NLS), a free service of the Library of Congress, is commonly referred to as Talking Books. NLS offers leisure materials and magazines on audiocassette or audiodisk. The collection includes popular novels, classical literature, poetry, biographies, and magazines. The Talking Books program has thousands of titles available or will order what the applicant requests. Talking Books are distributed through a network of regional and subregional libraries. There are no fees charged by the regional libraries of the NLS. Talking Books requires that your application be signed by a doctor of medicine, not a psychologist. Applications can be obtained from a Talking Books Center in your area.

Taped texts from both NLS and RFB&D require a special cassette player. The cassette player uses four-track tapes. The tape player is supplied as a free loan from NLS when you submit your application. A smaller sized version of the four-track player can be purchased through RFB&D and independent-living catalogs.

Variable Speech-Control Tape Recorders (VSCs) are portable units that, unlike standard/conventional tape recorders, enable the user to play back audiotape material (e.g., lectures, meetings, books on tape) slower or faster than the rate at which it was initially recorded, without the loss of intelligibility ("chipmunk"-like speech at faster speeds). Intelligible speech at varying rates is easily achieved by adjusting speed- and pitch-control levers. (Portions of this strategy are drawn from Raskind, 1994.)

Computer-Assisted Reading (CAR): There is software capability built into many computers, or it can be installed: To have text read aloud interactively (what you type is what you hear), a speech synthesizer, text-to-speech technology, is used. With this technology, you can have any text read back to you— text that you write or text that someone else has written.

• *Optical Character Recognition (OCR), including speech synthesis:*

OCR systems may be used to "read" material from hard copy (books, magazines, etc.). The system consists of a scanner, speech synthesizer with aid of software (i.e., screen reader software, which will read any text input or documented by the user), and computer. Users scan the material into the computer, which is, in turn, read aloud via the synthesizer as it is simultaneously highlighted on the screen. Options such as voice, rate of speech, and screen display may be individualized. These devices, originally designed for the visually impaired, may also be useful for persons with learning disabilities to circumvent difficulties with reading. If the user wants to use the reading machine with other software, such as word-processing programs, this will make standard applications, such as WordPerfect, talk to you. Speech synthesizers transform written text into spoken words (especially helpful to users with minimal reading skills). Text can be read back a letter, word, line, sentence, paragraph, or screen at a time.

- *Reading Machines (screen readers):* Reading machines are electronic devices that scan a printed page and, through a synthesized voice machine, read the printed material back to the user. Screen readers can be used for home, work, or school. Capabilities of the product can be expanded to suit the user's needs and require an electrical outlet. For reading and writing activities, students with learning disabilities may find screen reading/speech synthesis/highlighting systems useful. As the user types in data, a voice synthesizer speaks what is being typed at the same time the print is highlighted on the computer screen. In addition, reading machines scan printed materials and convert them to synthesized speech. Some reading machines can be interfaced with personal computers (the user can plug into a Macintosh, PC, or laptop), while others are stand-alone models that need only an electrical outlet. When purchase of a reading machine to be operated with a computer is being considered, the user should determine whether this technology will work with the user's system (most programs work only in DOS). It is also necessary to specify which version of Windows is loaded on your system.

- *Electronic Books/Books Published on Disk/E-Text:* Other than scanning, there are additional options for getting text into your computer. Once you have the electronic text on your machine, you can enlarge its type or have the machine read it to you. As described in the first strategy, RFB&D provides books copied to floppy disk for use with a computer. The floppy disks are available in either 3.5- or 5.25-inch format for IBM-compatible or Macintosh systems.

- *Screen-Magnification/Enlargement Software:* People with vision problems can have difficulty reading computer screens. Screen magnification helps them to be more productive. It is a useful tool in any situation where prolonged viewing of the screen might cause eyestrain and/or decreased productivity. There is software available that allows text to be magnified on screen. As well, alteration of colors on the screen is desirable, and individual preferences catered for, to make the viewing of text as comfortable as possible. Sometimes, changing font or print size makes the text more legible. Text may also be magnified by low-tech means, such as the use of closed-circuit television.

Written Language Difficulties

Problem: Students with written language disorders may have difficulty with grammar, punctuation, spelling, organization, and coherence. AT, especially computer-based programs, can simplify prewriting and revision processes and boost the creativity of students with writing difficulties.

Writing software can turn a PC or Macintosh into a voice-driven typewriter. With an additional card installed on a computer, the user speaks into a microphone instead of typing on the keyboard. Other aids allow the user to hear what is being written on the screen. Some programs use the computer's internal speakers to reproduce the words audibly, while others may require an external speech synthesizer.

Computer word processing lessens the stress about making errors, especially spelling. The cut-and-paste feature enhances coherence by allowing the writer to move words, sentences, and paragraphs within the text. This freedom can release persons with written language deficits from concern about the mechanics of writing, allowing them to redirect their efforts toward the meaning of their writing.

Students who have access to word processing have told me over and over again that they write more frequently than they did before they got their computers. Word processing also reduces the difficulties of writing by hand, and the computer gives a clear, accurate picture of what is written.

Word-processing software can also facilitate a sequential approach to writing when used with an accompanying outlining software. One of the most important areas in which word-processing software can help all students, including those with learning disabilities, is in the revision process. By electronically reorganizing the information through moving the text around, the student is able to write a draft and edit easily to make revisions. The student often experiences academic success and develops a sense of independence and pride in the work.

There are now new technological advances to help accommodate writing difficulties. These include tape recorders that compress voice onto a disk and transcribe it to print.

Writing Difficulties Strategies

Using Computers for Writing: The computer is an important element in the AT universe. Computer-based programs can assist persons with learning disabilities in activities involving reading and writing.

How a computer changes the writing process:

- The computer eliminates handwriting problems.
- Proofreading is easier because the text is more legible.
- The writer may experience less frustration, including anxiety, than when using pen and paper.

- The writer may experience fewer difficulties with vocabulary and reasoning.
- Spelling and mechanics can be de-emphasized and moved to the end of the writing process.
- Outlining and organization are easier by cutting and pasting.

Beginning users will find the Macintosh family of computers easier to learn. Many of the software processes are simple and intuitive. On-screen icons, small pictures representing a range of activities, simplify the process. The user needs only to point and click to open a program application.

Now that Microsoft Windows is available, an IBM-compatible computer (PC) can function in much the same way as a Macintosh. Windows is a software program that interfaces the user with the disk operating system (DOS) on IBM and compatible computers. Windows software requires a PC with system 286 or higher.

It is imperative that persons with learning disabilities choose computer systems and software programs that operate with Windows or one of the Macintosh family of computers. The icons on these more advanced machines are a significant accommodation for persons with learning disabilities.

Word-Processing Programs: Word processing is a method by which persons with learning disabilities and other impairments can produce written documents without many of the barriers they face with conventional writing methods. In a word-processing program, typewritten text gives a clear, accurate picture of what is written. Word-processing programs work hand in hand with other computer software writing aids. These aids help with outlining, revising, predicting words, checking grammar and spelling, developing vocabulary, and highlighting words and phrases.

Word Abbreviation and Expansion Programs

- *Intelligent Word-Prediction Programs* help poor spellers to write. Users who use a speech-recognition program need only to speak the word; those lacking a speech-recognition program must spell out the first few letters. In either case, a list is displayed of the most likely words. The user needs only to have the word entered into the text.

- *Predictive Word Processors* offer valuable support to learners for whom every word is achieved with difficulty. They offer a selection of likely words to follow what has been typed already, so the user selects the most appropriate word with a single keystroke. The more sophisticated programs allow the user to add personal words to the list.

- *Word Abbreviation/Expansion Programs* allow the writer to (1) use preestablished abbreviations (e.g., typing "ASAP" produces "as soon as possible" in the text) or (2) customize abbreviations for words, phrases, and sentences as computer commands (e.g., "LD" yields "learning disabilities.") The writer, in other words, recalls the word(s) by using an abbreviation. Such programs enable persons with limited keyboard skills to increase typing speed.

Speech-Recognition Software: These programs enable text to appear on the computer screen as the user speaks into a microphone, rather than typing on the keyboard. Such programs are compatible with word-processing programs.

Other Software Writing Programs

- *Spell-Checking Programs:* These may be useful to even the most competent speller. To a hesitant speller, they can be invaluable. Spell-checking software checks for correct spelling of words in a document; each incorrect spelling is compared to the dictionary file, and an alternative spelling is offered. Spell checkers do not alert for inappropriately used words. If the word is spelled correctly, it will not be flagged. Therefore, it is important to proofread the document for inappropriate word use or to use grammar-checking software, which will alert the user to incorrect usage and offer alternatives.

- *Outlining/Brainstorming Software:* Many persons with learning disabilities have difficulty organizing topics, categories, and sequence. An appropriate method for many adult students with learning disabilities is to allow them to "dump" any ideas on paper without regard to organization. Outlining programs allow the user to dump information in an unstructured manner; this information can subsequently be placed in appropriate categories and ordered more easily. An outlining program assists in planning and organizing a document by creating outline headings, subheadings, and key points

- *Free-Form Databases:* These software programs enable the user to create his or her own notes, of any length, on any subject. Rather than notes on paper, these electronically stored notes can be retrieved by typing in any piece of information contained in the note. The ability to retrieve information by only remembering a fragment or piece of information contained within the note can be quite beneficial for individuals with memory and organizational difficulties. Through a simple cursor movement that highlights a keyword or phrase within each note, the user can browse through all the notes within the data base until the one being sought is found.
- *Encyclopedias* on computer are available on CD-ROM or Internet on-line services. Depending on the product, one can get options for speech (the research source is read to the user) and size of print. The user who experiences difficulty with comprehension due to decoding may circumvent or bypass this area by listening to the articles read aloud. (Portions of this strategy were drawn form Raskind, 1993, 1994.)

Electronic Assistive Technology (Not Computer-based):
Hand-held electronic devices, such as dictionaries, encyclopedias, spell checkers, and a thesaurus, are useful for students and workers as they move about, without access to a computer. Audiocassette recorders may also be used for note taking.

Portable Keyboards: Portable keyboards are pieces of equipment that can be carried around. They enable students to practice keyboarding in addition to writing and electronically storing reports, essays, and notes without having to be at a computer. The stored information can be either printed or transferred from the keyboard to a desktop or laptop. Portable keyboards are a nice way to introduce students to computers.

Math Difficulties

Problem: Math difficulties can be a challenge to remediate and/or accommodate. Many students with disabilities have histories of academic failure that contribute to the development of learned helplessness in math. Students may practice computing division facts but do not understand what division means. This lack of understanding fosters their dependency on the teacher and promotes the belief that external help is needed to solve problems correctly. People with learning disabilities who have math problems usually have visual perception difficulties, which affect their ability to see likenesses and differences in shape and form.

They may experience conceptual problems with the following:

- Measurements: What is a 2 by 4? Is a quarter of an inch smaller than three-sixteenths?
- Volume: Is a half-cup larger than a fourth-cup?
- Computation symbols: What is 37×3? What is $1/16 \div 3/7$?

Because math symbols represent a way to express numerical language concepts, language skills become very important to math achievement. Many students with learning disabilities have reading difficulties that interfere with their ability to solve word problems. The fear of failure and low self-esteem cause students to become so tense that their ability to solve problems and to learn or apply math concepts is impaired. Confused thinking, disorganization, avoidance behavior, and math phobia are common results.

The technology for remediating and accommodating persons with math disabilities has not developed as readily as the technology for reading and writing. However, the technology that is available now can provide beneficial assistance for some problems.

The limited technology can be of help, especially to those who have problems writing numbers down in the correct order. The most common, currently available tools include the following:

- Hand-held calculators, which can help a learner who has problems writing numbers in the correct order
- Talking calculators, which vocalize data and resulting calculations through speech synthesis
- Special-feature calculators, which enable the user to select options to speak and simultaneously display numbers, functions, entire equations, and results
- On-screen computer calculator programs with speech synthesis
- Large display screens for calculators and adding machines
- Color-coding for maintaining columns
- Big number buttons and large keypads
- Textbooks on CD-ROM
- Videotaped math lessons

Computer-assisted instruction (CAI) math courses (instruction targeted to special students) are being developed. These are particularly helpful to the user with learning disabilities, if the learning is reinforced with voice output.

Daily-Living and Social Skills Difficulties

Problem: Daily-living and social skills are often disregarded as elements of learning disabilities. Some people have more difficulty than others in environments less structured than school and work.

Some students with learning disabilities face challenges in their day-to-day activities besides the more familiar writing, reading, and math problems. These highly documented academic problems clearly permeate the lives of students with learning disabilities and have a significant impact on daily living. But there are challenges that will arise within the course of daily living and in social interaction.

Daily living requires the fulfillment of many tasks, like conceptualizing directions; reading maps, signs, and menus; dialing phone numbers; filling out job applications; playing board games and cards; telling time; staying abreast of current news; managing personal information; staying on-task; purchasing retail items; managing time; scheduling and keeping appointments; and, in general, organizing their lives.

The absence of social skills is also a disability. Everyone, from time to time, experiences deep discomfort in social situations, especially students with learning disabilities. This discomfort often arises from the individual's low self-esteem and a lack of self-confidence. For example, Jonathan's reluctance to raise his hand in class could be a direct result of his struggles growing up with learning disabilities. He may think that he is not smart enough or capable of asking a question or expressing himself in front of others.

But there is another level that may be affecting Jonathan, one in which lack of social skills is based not only on low self-esteem or self-confidence, but also on neurological impairments, which affect his ability to perceive nonverbal cues. For example, Mary is a teenager trying to get a part-time job. During her interviews, she speaks too loudly and avoids eye contact; she asks personal questions of the interviewer, rambles about her own personal life, and strays far afield when she is asked direct questions. To Mary, her behavior appears appropriate, but her disability prevents her from recognizing her inappropriate social behavior.

Common manifestations of this social disability may include the following: clumsiness; lack of eye contact; asking inappropriate or blunt questions and giving the same type of responses; inability to control voice volume and tone; and failure to "take turns" in conversation, to initiate conversations, to form healthy relationships with family and friends, to date, to maintain personal hygiene, to dress appropriately for the occasion, and many others.

AT remains limited in these areas. What high-tech tools are on the market to assist organization and social skills appear below.

Strategies to Enhance Daily-Living and Social Skills Difficulties

- *Headphones or earplugs* to shut out distractions and enhance concentration while reading or writing are beneficial to persons with attention deficit hyperactivity disorder (ADHD).

- *Amplification* for students with learning disabilities improves listening conditions and attention levels by amplifying the instructor's voice and reducing the effects of background noise. A typical product is composed of two basic parts: a wireless transmitter with a microphone (worn by the instructor) and a receiver with headset or earphone (worn by the student). The system carries the speaker's voice directly from the speaker's mouth to the listener's ear, helping to make the speaker's voice more prominent. This device improves auditory discrimination and auditory attention by allowing the individual to focus on the speaker, overriding extraneous and distracting background noise.

- *Personal Data Managers* are available as software programs. Typical features include monthly calendars, daily schedules, planners, a clock and alarm, memo files, "to do" lists, address books, telephone directories, and check registers. Personal data managers allow the user to store, organize, and retrieve vast amounts of personal information, which is useful for persons with organizational and/or memory difficulties.

- *Free-Form Databases* are software programs that enable the user to create his or her own notes of any length, on any subject. Rather than notes on paper, these electronically stored notes can be retrieved by typing in any piece of information contained within the note. The ability to retrieve information by remembering only a fragment or piece of information can be quite beneficial for individuals with memory and organizational difficulties. Through a simple cursor movement that highlights each note, the user can browse through all the notes within the data base until the one being sought is found (Raskind 1993).

- *Interactive CD-ROM Programs* are the most effective media for assisting those persons with social skills difficulties. They enable the user to role play in simulations of real-life situations and to place the user in decision-making positions.

Conclusion

It is our intent that the AT strategies discussed in this chapter will give you a user-friendly overview of some of the tools that are being used to help students with learning disabilities become more independent and productive. Due to the nature of this book, we have chosen not to get into specific individual products. In most of the areas discussed, there is a variety of products from which to choose. It is important to keep in mind that word-of-mouth is the best way to find out about the effectiveness of a product. In researching products, it is important that you consider the following points:

- The nature of the disability
- The individual's knowledge about technology
- The cost of the adaptive software and equipment
- The time it takes to learn how to use the adaptive software and equipment
- The compatibility of the adaptive software and equipment with your computer
- The technical support offered by the manufacturer
- The technical manuals in accessible format
- The portability of the adaptive software and equipment
- The cross-setting capabilities of the adaptive software and equipment

When appropriate, school systems should provide AT evaluations. These evaluations will offer specific AT suggestions for students, which should be included in their education plans and be monitored and reviewed on a regular basis. When possible, try before you buy. Due to the expense and learning curve of most technology, it is a good idea to locate equipment to try out before you buy it. Most states have limited equipment loan libraries that might be helpful. You may also want to contact the Alliance on Technology Access (ATA) Center in your area, which may have adaptive software and equipment for you to try out.

It might be helpful to develop an individual AT solution plan for some students. This plan could include instructional areas, modifications, standard tools, and AT solutions. Table 8-1 is an example of an AT solution plan developed by the Georgia Project for Assistive Technology (GPAT). A chart such as this should be a working document that changes as the student's needs change.

Works Cited

Cunningham, C., and N. Coombs. 1997. *Information Access and Adaptive Technology*. Phoenix: Oryx Press.

Raskind, M. H. 1993. *Assistive Technology for Adults with Learning Disabilities: A Rationale for Use*. Los Angeles: The Frostig Center.

Table 8-1 *Assistive Technology Solution Chart: Frequently Used Modifications as Assistive Technology Solutions for Instruction and Access**

Instructional or Access Area	Modifications of Task Expectations	Standard Tools	Assistive Technology Solutions
Writing	• Increased time for completing assignments • Decreased length of assignment/number of responses • Oral diction as an alternative to writing • Peer notetaker • Format of assignment changed to multiple choice, fill-in-the-blank • Webbing-concept mapping strategy	• Crayon/marker • Pencil • Pen • Typewriter • Computer with word-processing software • Assorted types of paper (lined, color, graph) • Plastic writing guides • Line-by-line writing	• Pencil grip or other adapted grip • Adapted paper (bold line, raised line, different spacing, secured to desk, paper stabilizers) • Slate board • No-slip writing surface • Tape recorder • Portable word processor (e.g., PC-5, Alpha Smart, etc.) • Notetaking device (e.g., Braille, adapted tape recorder) • Computer with word-processing software with adaptive input hardware and/or software (e.g., keyguard, keyboard utilities, enlarged keyboard, touchscreen, trackball, switch access, word-prediction software, voice dictation software, Braille input, etc.) • Computer with word-processing software and appropriate output software (e.g., screen enlargement, screen reading software, etc.)

Table 8-1 (*continued*)

Instructional or Access Area	Modifications of Task Expectations	Standard Tools	Assistive Technology Solutions
			• Computer with appropriate process and editing tools (outlining software, multimedia software, grammar and spell checkers, talking word processors)
Spelling	• Peer/adult assistance for difficult to spell words • Personal or custom dictionary • Problem word list • Reduce number or spelling errors • Increased time for completing assignments	• Print dictionary • Instructional software to enhance phonics and spelling skills • Computer with word-processing software with built-in spell checker	• Tape recorder with difficult-to-spell words recorded • Hand-held spell checker without auditory output • Hand-held spell checker with auditory recognition of entered word • Portable word processor with built-in spell checker • Computer with word-processing program and adaptive features (talking spell checker, word-prediction software, etc.) • Word prediction/abbreviation programs
Reading	• Peer/adult reading • High interest, lower reading-level materials	• Textbooks • Work sheets • Printed information board	• Reading aids (e.g., talking spell checker or dictionary as a word-recognition aid, etc.)

Table 8-1 (continued)

Instructional or Access Area	Modifications of Task Expectations	Standard Tools	Assistive Technology Solutions
	• Increased time for completing reading materials • Decreased length of assignment • Simplify text • Review table of contents • Graphic organizer	• Printed test materials • Instructional software to remediate or enhance basic reading and/or reading comprehension skills • Colored transparencies • Large print	• Electronic books (e.g., disk or CD-ROM) • Alternatives or supplements to printed information (e.g., tape-recorded or talking books; computer-based, talking, word-processing program with adaptive input as needed; screen-reading software with adaptive input as needed) • Solutions for converting text into alternative format (e.g., scanner with OCT software)
Math	• Change format of assignment (e.g., write answers only) • Peer/adult reading of problem and recording of answer • Reduce number of problems	• Manipulative (beads, etc.) • Abacus • Number line • Math fact sheet (e.g., multiplication facts) • Calculator with print output • Instructional software to enhance and remediate math skills	• Modified paper (e.g., graph; enlarged, raised line; etc.) • Talking calculator with speech output • Calculator with large print display • Calculator with large keypad • Computer-based on-screen calculator • Electronic math work sheet software with adaptive input and output as needed (e.g., MathPad, Access to Math, and Study Works)

Table 8-1 *(continued)*

Instructional or Access Area	Modifications of Task Expectations	Standard Tools	Assistive Technology Solutions
			• Adapted measuring devices (e.g., devices with speed output, large print display, tactile output)
Study Skills	• Assignment sheet provided by peer/adult • Outlines of key points • Online homework	• Instructional materials, including software to remediate deficit areas, to teach compensation strategies, and to focus on strengths institutions	• Print or picture schedule • Organizational aids (e.g., color-coding, appointment book, etc.) • Tape recorder • Computer-based electronic organizer with adapted input and output provided as needed • Speech-prompting device
Oral Communication		• Organizing diagram for presentations	• Speech-enhancing devices (e.g., amplifiers, clarifiers) • Augmentative communication solutions (e.g., object-based communication displays, picture communication boards, books, wallets, talking switches, dedicated augmentative communication devices, and integrated, computer-based augmentative communication solutions—all with adaptive input as needed)

* This document was developed by the Georgia Project for Assistive Technology (328 Forest Parkway, Suite C, Forest Park, GA 30297), 1998, and is not reproducible for classroom use.

Appendix

Resources

Advocacy Resources

American Association for Adult & Continuing Education (AAACE)
AAACE
4380 Forbes Blvd.
Lanham, MD 20706
Phone: 202-429-5131
Web site: http://www.cdlr.tamu.edu/tcall/aaace/
This organization provides leadership for the field of adult and continuing education by expanding opportunities for adult growth and development.

American Association of People with Disabilities (AAPD)
AAPD Member Services
P. O. Box 97045
Washington, DC 20091-7045
Phone: 888-712-4672
Web site: http://www.aapd.com/
This organization is a nonprofit, nonpartisan, cross-disability organization whose goals are unity, leadership, and impact.

American Council on Education
One DuPont Circle
Washington, DC 20036
Phone: 202-939-9480
Toll Free: 800-626-9433
Web site: http://www.acenet.edu/
This council is dedicated to the belief that equal educational opportunity and a strong higher education system are essential cornerstones of a democratic society. ACE is a forum for the discussion of major issues related to higher education and its potential to contribute to the quality of American life.

GEDTS, a division of the American Council on Education, administers the GED tests and provides information on disability-related adaptations/accommodations for the GED tests to prospective examinees and instructors. Successful GED test takers earn a high school equivalency diploma. The tests are available in audio, Braille, and large-print editions. GEDTS also publishes *GED Items*, a bi-monthly newsletter for examiners and the Materials Development Center for adult education instructors.

American Speech-Language-Hearing Association (ASLHA)
10801 Rockville Pike
Rockville, MD 20852
Phone: 301-897-5700 (voice or TTY)

Phone: 800-638-8255
Fax: 301-571-0457
E-mail: actioncenter@aslha.org
Web site: http://www.aslha.org
This organization promotes and provides the highest quality of services for professionals in audiology, speech-language pathology, and speech, language, and hearing science, and is an advocate for people with communication disabilities.

A.D.D. WareHouse
300 Northwest 70th Avenue, Suite 102
Plantation, FL 33317
Phone: 800-233-9273
Phone: 954-792-8100
Fax: 954-792-8545
Web site: http://www.addwarehouse.com
This organization is a resource for the understanding and treatment of all developmental disorders, including attention deficit hyperactivity disorder (ADHD) and related disorders.

Association for the Advancement of Rehabilitative Technology (RESNA)
1700 North Moore Street, Suite 1540
Arlington, VA 22209-1903
Phone: 703-524-6686
TTY: 703-524-6639
Fax: 703-524-6630
E-mail: info@resna.org
Web site: http://www.resna.org
This organization improves the potential of people with disabilities to achieve their goals through the use of technology.

Center on Disabilities
California State University (CSUN), Northridge
18111 Nordhoff Street
Northridge, CA 91330-8340
Phone, V/TDD, message: 818-885-2578
Fax: 818-885-4929
E-mail: LTM@csun.edu
Web site: http://www.csun.edu/cod/
The Center is committed to providing outstanding student services to students with disabilities, and to making a contribution to the field of disabilities in general and to those who provide services to people with disabilities by the dissemination of information through training programs, conferences, workshops, seminars, and electronic media, and may also conduct applications-oriented research as a means of improving the lives of persons with disabilities and the professional skills of those who work with them.

Children and Adults with Attention-Deficit/Hyperactivity Disorder (CHADD)
499 Northwest 70th Avenue, Suite 308
Plantation, FL 33317
Phone: 305-587-3700
Web site: http://www.chadd.or.org/
This organization is dedicated to working with children and adults with attention-deficit/hyperactivity disorder.

Closing the Gap
P. O. Box 68
Henderson, MN 56044
Phone: 507-248-3294
Fax: 507-248-3810
Closing the Gap Newsletter reviews software products appropriate for handicapped and disabled persons and explains in everyday language how this technology is being successfully implemented in education, rehabilitation, and vocational settings around the world. The newsletter costs $29.00 in the United States, $44 in Canada and Mexico, and $60 overseas.

Council for Exceptional Children (CEC)
P. O. Box 79026
Baltimore, MD 21279-0026.
Phone: 800-328-0272
Web site: http://www.cec.sped.org/mb/join.htm
This Council is dedicated to improving educational outcomes for individuals with exceptionalities, students with disabilities, and/or the gifted.

DO-IT Disabilities
University of Washington
Box 354842
Seattle, WA 98195-4842
Phone (voice/TTY): 206-685-DOIT (3648)
Fax: 206-221-4171
E-mail: doit@u.washington.edu
Web site: http://www.washington.edu/doit/
Programs to promote the use of technology to maximize the independence, productivity, and participation of people with disabilities.

Disability Resource Associates (DRA)
587 Virginia Avenue, #607
Atlanta, GA 30306
Phone: 404-408-5988
Web site: http://disabilityresource.org
An organization that offers motivational training and information on disabilities issues, including disabilities awareness, learning disabilities, development of self-advocacy skills, and assistive technology.

EASI (Equal Access to Software and Information)
P. O. Box 18928
Rochester, NY 14618
Phone: 716-244-9065
Fax: 716-475-7120
E-mail: easi@educom.edu
Web site: http://www.rit.edu/~easi
EASI's mission is to serve as a resource to the education community by providing information and guidance in the area of access-to-information technologies by individuals with disabilities. They stay informed about developments and advancements within the adaptive computer technology field and spread that information to colleges, universities, K–12 schools, libraries, and the workplace.

Eaton Coull Learning Group, Ltd.
3541 West 16th Avenue
Vancouver, BC
Canada V6R 3C2
Phone: 604-734-5588
Phone: 800-933-4063
Fax: 604-734-5510
The Eaton Coull Learning Group, Ltd. develops and produces educational products for individuals of all learning styles, with an emphasis on resources for people with learning disabilities and/or attention deficit disorder.

Faking It: A Look into the Mind of a Creative Learner Home Page
Phone: 404-815-0045
E-mail: christopherlee@mindspring.com
E-mail: rjackson@mail.gcsu.edu
Web site: http://accucomm.net/~rjackson/
This site gives information on Christopher Lee and Rosemary Jackson, Ph.D.

HEATH Resource Center (National Clearinghouse on Postsecondary Education for Individuals with Disabilities; American Council on Education)
c/o HEATH Resource Center
One DuPont Circle, NW, Suite 800
Washington, DC 20036
Phone: 202-939-9320
Phone: 800-544-3284
Fax: 202-833-4760
Web site: http://www.acenet.edu/programs/HEATH/home.html
The HEATH Resource Center operates the National Clearinghouse on Postsecondary Education for individuals with disabilities. A program of the American Council on Education, HEATH serves as an information exchange for the educational support services, policies, procedures, adaptations, and opportunities of American campuses, vocational–technical schools, adult education programs, and other training entities after high school. The Center collects and disseminates this information so that people with disabilities can develop their full potential through postsecondary education and training.

International Dyslexia Association (formerly Orton Dyslexia Society)
8600 LaSalle Road, Chester Building, Suite 382
Baltimore, MD 21286-2044
Phone: 800-222-3123
Fax: 410-321-5069
Web site: http://interds.org/
This organization promotes effective teaching approaches and related clinical, educational intervention strategies for dyslexics. The Society is an international scientific and educational association concerned with the widespread problem of the specific language disability of developmental dyslexia. Local state chapters serve as literacy resources for dyslexic adults and those who teach or advise them. Annual membership: $55.00.

Job Accommodation Network (JAN)
c/o West Virginia University
P. O. Box 6080
Morgantown, WV 26506-6080

Phone: 800-526-7234
TTY: 800-526-7234 (V/TTY)
Web site: http://janweb.icdi.wvu.edu/
The Job Accommodation Network (JAN) is an international toll-free consulting service that provides information about job accommodations and the employability of people with functional limitations. The mission of JAN is to assist in the hiring, retraining, retention, or advancement of persons with disabilities by providing accommodation information. Anyone may call JAN for information. Calls are answered by consultants who understand the functional limitations associated with disabilities, and who have instant access to the most comprehensive and up-to-date information about accommodation methods, devices, and strategies.

Laubach Literacy Action (LLA)

P. O. Box 131
1320 Jamesville Avenue
Syracuse, NY 132210
Phone: 315-422-9121
This organization is a committed partner in a national effort to help all people reach their full literate potential.

Learning Disabilities Association of America (LDA)

4156 Library Road
Pittsburgh, PA 15234-1349
Phone: 412-341-1515
Web site: http://www.ldanatl.org/
LDA is a nonprofit volunteer advocacy organization, and provides information and referral for parents, professionals, and consumers involved with or in search of support groups and networking opportunities through local LDA Youth and Adult Section chapters.

A publication list is available. The Association also prints *LDA Newsbriefs*, a bimonthly newsletter for parents, professionals, and adults with learning disabilities.

Alabama Learning Disabilities Association	334-277-9151
Arizona Learning Disabilities Association	602-495-1175
Arkansas Learning Disabilities Association	501-666-8777
District of Columbia Learning Disabilities Association	202-667-9140
Florida Learning Disabilities Association	941-637-8957
Georgia Learning Disabilities Association	404-514-8088
Illinois Learning Disabilities Association	708-430-7532
Indiana Learning Disabilities Association	317-898-5751
Iowa Learning Disabilities Association	515-961-6413
Louisiana Learning Disabilities Association	318-357-5154
Maine Learning Disabilities Association	207-582-2866
Maryland Learning Disabilities Association	410-265-8188
Michigan Learning Disabilities Association	517-485-8160
Mississippi Learning Disabilities Association	601-982-2812
Montana Learning Disabilities Association	406-252-7716
Nebraska Learning Disabilities Association	402-571-7771
New Hampshire Learning Disabilities Association	603-429-0648
New Jersey Learning Disabilities Association	908-571-1221
New Mexico Learning Disabilities Association	505-821-2545
New York Learning Disabilities Association	518-436-4633

North Carolina Learning Disabilities Association	919-493-5362
North Dakota Learning Disabilities Association	710-224-2671
Ohio Learning Disabilities Association	216-273-7388
Oklahoma Learning Disabilities Association	405-743-1366
Rhode Island Learning Disabilities Association	401-232-3822
South Carolina Learning Disabilities Association	803-926-8302
Texas Learning Disabilities Association	512-458-8234
Vermont Learning Disabilities Association	802-362-3127
Virginia Learning Disabilities Association	804-842-9305
Washington Learning Disabilities Association	206-882-0820
West Virginia Learning Disabilities Association	304-344-0252
Wisconsin Learning Disabilities Association	414-821-0855

L. D. Adults of Georgia
P. O. Box 1337
Roswell, GA 30077
State Office Phone: 770-514-8088
Web site: http://www.gatfl.org/ld/
L. D. Adults of Georgia is a nonprofit organization that is affiliated with the Learning Disabilities Association of Georgia and the national organization, Learning Disabilities Association of America.

LD Online
Web site: http://www.ldonline.org
This on-line guide offers a vast array of information on topics within the area of learning disabilities. Here you'll find articles written by the leading experts, research findings reported by top researchers, and the latest news in the field of learning disabilities.

LD Resources
Web site: http://www.ldresources.com/
This organization has provided information on technology for learning disabilities since 1995. The site is hosted by HostPro and is built on a Macintosh with TexEdit Plus.

Library Service for the Blind & Physically Handicapped
901 G Street NW, Room 215
Washington, DC 20001
Librarian: Grace J. Lyons
Phone: 800-424-8567
Phone: 202-727-2142
TDD: 202-727-2145
Fax: 202-727-1129
E-mail: dclalyons@hotmail.com
Web site: http://dclibrary.org/lbph/
This library administers a free library program of Braille and recorded materials, circulated to eligible borrowers through a network of cooperating libraries.

National Adult Literacy and Learning Disabilities Center (National ALLD Center)
National ALLD Center
Academy for Educational Development
1875 Connecticut Avenue, NW
Washington, DC 20009-1202
Phone: 202-884-8185

Phone: 800-953-2553
Fax: 202-884-8429
Internet: info@nalidc.aed.org
Web site: http://novel.nifl.gov/nalidtop.htm
The National ALLD Center is funded by the National Institute for Literacy under a cooperative agreement with the Academy for Educational Development in collaboration with the University of Kansas Institute for Research in Learning Disabilities.

National Center for Learning Disabilities (NCLD)
381 Park Avenue, South
Suite 1420
New York, NY 10016
Phone: 212-545-7510
Fax: 212-545-9665
NCLD is an organization committed to improving the lives of those affected by learning disabilities. NCLD provides services and conducts programs nationwide, benefiting children and adults with learning disabilities, their families, teachers, and other professionals. NCLD provides the latest information on learning disabilities and local resources to parents, professionals, employers, and others dealing with learning disabilities. NCLD's annual publication is *Their World*.

National Information Center for Children & Youth with Handicaps (NICCYH)
P. O. Box 1492
Washington, DC 20013-1492
Phone (voice/TTY): 800-695-0285
Phone (voice/TTY): 202-884-8200
Fax: 202-884-8441
E-mail: nichcy@aed.org
Web site: http://www.nichcy.org
NICCYH is the national information and referral center that provides information on disabilities and disability-related issues for families, educators, and other professionals. This research and training center is dedicated to the study and promotion of the psychological and social well being of children with chronic conditions and their families.

National Institute on Disability and Rehabilitation Research
400 Maryland Avenue, SW
Washington, DC 20202-2572
Phone: 202-205-8134
TTY: 202-205-9433
Phone: 202-205-8189
Web site: http://www.ed.gov/offices/OSERS/NIDRR/
The United States Department of Education's Office of Special Education and Rehabilitative Services (OSERS), through its National Institute on Disability and Rehabilitation Research (NIDRR), conducts comprehensive and coordinated programs of research and related activities to maximize the full inclusion, social integration, employment, and independent living of disabled individuals of all ages. Balanced between the scientific and consumer communities, NIDRR plays a unique role in federally funded research activities. In addition, NIDRR's work helps to more fully integrate disability research into the mainstream of our nation's policies regarding science and technology, health care, and economics.

159

National Library Service for the Blind and Physically Handicapped (NLS)
Library of Congress
Washington, DC 20542
Phone: 202-707-5100
Fax: 202-707-0712
Web site: http://lcweb.kic.gov/nis/
NLS, Library of Congress administers a free library program of Braille and recorded materials circulated to eligible borrowers through a network of cooperating libraries. Browse the library address list to locate the regional or subregional library closest to the eligible individual. Contact the library by phone, fax, or in writing and request an application for service. If you are unable to locate a library or wish additional assistance, send a message via e-mail or call 202-707-5100.

One A.D.D. Place
Web site: http://www.oneaddplace.com/
A virtual neighborhood consolidation in one place; information and resources relating to attention deficit disorder (ADD), AD/D, and learning disorders (LD).

President's Committee for Employment of People with Disabilities
1331 F. Street, NW
Washington, DC 20004
Phone: 202-376-6200
Web site: http://www50.pcepd.gov/pcepd/
The President's Committee is a small federal agency whose chairman and vice chairs are appointed by the President. The chairman appoints the other Executive Board members and members of the six standing subcommittees. Directed by the chairman and Executive Board, the Committee achieves its goals through the work of its subcommittee members and a thirty-seven-member agency staff, in close cooperation with the Governors' Committees in the states, Puerto Rico, Virgin Islands, and Guam, and with Mayor's Committees throughout the United States.

Recordings for the Blind & Dyslexic (RFB&D)
20 Roszel Road
Princeton, NJ 20542
Phone: 609-452-0606
Phone: 800-221-4792
Web site: http://www.rfbd.org
This organization serves nearly 78,000 people with "print disabilities" (which include blindness, visual impairments, learning disabilities, or other physical disabilities), and has titles available for students in kindergarten through postgraduate studies. RFB&D is a national nonprofit organization that provides taped educational books free on loan, books on diskette, library services, and other educational and professional resources to individuals who cannot read standard print because of a visual, physical, or perceptual disability.

Rehabilitation Engineering and Assistive Technology Society of North America (RESNA)
RESNA
1700 N. Moore Street, Suite 1540
Arlington, VA 22209-1903
Phone: 703-524-6686
TTY: 703-524-6639

Fax: 703-524-6630

Web site: http://www.resna.org/

RESNA is an interdisciplinary association of people with a common interest in technology and disability. Its purpose is to improve the potential of people with disabilities to achieve their goals through the use of technology. That purpose is served by promoting research, development, education, advocacy, and the provision of technology, and by supporting the people engaged in these activities. RESNA was founded in 1979 as a not-for-profit professional organization. There are currently over 1,600 individual and 150 organizational members.

Tools for Life (TFL)

2 Peachtree Street NW, Suite 35-415

Atlanta, GA 30303

Phone: 404-657-3084

Web site: http://www.gatfl.org/

Tools for Life increases access to appropriate assistive technology (AT) devices and services for people with disabilities so they can live, learn, work, and play independently in communities of their choice.

TRACE Research and Development Center

S-151 Weisman Center

1500 Highland Avenue

Madison, WI 53705

Phone: 608-262-6966

TDD: 608-262-5408

E-mail: essers@macc.wisc.edu

Vocational Independence Program (VIP)

New York Institute of Technology

P. O. Box 8000

Old Westbury, NY 11568-8000

Phone: 516-686-7516, 800-345-NYIT (6948)

Web site: http://www.nyit.edu/admissions/welcome.html

This program is designed for students with significant learning disabilities. It offers twenty vocational majors and places students on an associate or bachelor degree track. Students are full-time residents and have the opportunity to participate in the full range of student life.

World Institute on Disability

510 16th Street

Oakland, CA 94612-1500

Phone: 510-763-4100

TTY: 510-208-9493

Fax: 510-763-4109

The World Institute on Disability (WID) is a public policy, research, and training center dedicated to independence for all people with disabilities.

Vendor Resources

Advantage Learning Systems, Inc.

P. O. Box 8036

Wisconsin Rapids, WI 54495

Phone: 888-656-2931
This organization provides K–12 schools with computerized learning-information systems: software and related training designed to improve academic performance by increasing the quality, quantity, and timeliness of information in the classroom.

American Guidance Service (AGS)
4201 Woodland Road
Circle Pines, MN 55014
Phone: 800-328-2560
This organization is the leading publisher of assessments, textbooks, and instructional materials for students with a wide ability range.

American Printing House for the Blind
1839 Frankfort Avenue
Louisville, KY 40206-0085
Phone: 800-223-1839
The world's largest company devoted solely to making products for the blind.

Arkenstone, Inc.
11800 31st Court North
St. Petersburg, FL 33716
Phone: 800-444-4443
This organization focuses on changing the world for people with sensory and learning disabilities by creating innovative assistive technology products and solutions.

Articulate Systems
52 Third Avenue
Burlington, MA 01803
Phone: 617-935-5656
This organization focuses on breaking down language barriers through advanced translation technology, and on enabling people to interact by voice—in any language—with the machines that empower them.

Aurora Systems
P. O. Box 43005
Burnaby, BC
V5G-3H0 Canada
Phone: 888-290-1133
This organization provides affordable, effective assistance to people with special needs.

CompassLearning (formerly Jostens Learning)
9920 Pacific Heights Boulevard
San Diego, CA 92121
Phone: 800-244-0575
This organization is the leading provider of instructional software, with over seven thousand hours of instruction. More than twenty thousand schools, serving nearly fourteen million students, use CompassLearning programs designed to help teachers manage student performance, personalize learning, and connect communities of learners.

Dragon Systems
320 Nevada Street
Newton, MA 02460
Phone: 800-825-5897

162

This organization provides more than fifty-eight thousand visually and physically disabled people with free services offered by the Braille and Talking Book Library.

Henter-Joyce
11800 31st Court North
St. Petersburg, FL 33716
Phone: 800-336-5658
This organization seeks to change the world for individuals with learning disabilities by creating innovative assistive technology products and solutions.

Humanware, Inc.
6245 King Road
Loomis, CA 95650
Phone: 916-652-7253
This organization specializes in assistive technology for persons who have difficulties reading print due to blindness, low vision, or learning and/or reading disabilities.

Independent Living Aids, Inc.
27 East Mall
Plainview NY 11803-4404
Phone: 800-537-2118
Web site: http:/www.independentliving.com
Independent Living Aids, Inc., is a source for Hi-Tech, Lo-Tech for people with disabilities.

Inspiration Software, Inc.
7412 SW Beaverton Hillsdale Highway, Suite 102
Portland, OR 97225-2167
Phone: 503-245-9011
This corporation focuses on the development and support of visual learning and thinking tools in order to provide quality products and services for the education market.

Intellitools
1720 Corporate Circle
Petaluma, CA 94954
Phone: 800-899-6687
This organization provides high-quality adaptive computer products that are affordable and innovative and that also help people learn, communicate, and live to their fullest potential.

isSound (formerly Productivity Works, Inc.)
830 Bear Tavern Road, Suite 301
Ewing NJ 08628
Phone: 609-637-0099
This company is a provider and developer of software products for the auditory enabling of both applications and Web devices.

James Stanfield Publishing, Inc.
Drawer WEB
P. O. Box 41058
Santa Barbara, CA 93140
Phone: 800-421-6534
This organization offers the most respected library of educational materials available today in the areas of conflict management for the general school population and for students with cognitive challenges.

The Learning Company (formerly Microsystems Software, Inc.)
11800 31st Court North
St. Petersburg, FL 33716-1805
Phone: 800-336-5658
This company no longer markets or supports the Handiware line of adaptive access products originally developed by Microsystems Software.

Lighthouse, Inc.
111 E. 59th St.
New York, NY 10022-1202
Phone: 800-829-0500
This organization specializes in the rental and sales of lighting and control equipment and supplies for the film, video, and photographic industries in Minneapolis.

MathSoft, Inc.
101 Main Street
Cambridge, MA 02142-1521
Phone: 800-628-4223
This company is the leading provider of math, science, and engineering software for business, academia, research, and government.

Prentke Romich Company
1022 Heyl Road
Wooster, OH 44691
Phone: 800-262-1984
This company is the world-wide leader in the development and manufacture of augmentative communication devices, computer access products, and other assistive technology for people with severe disabilities.

Pro-Ed
8700 Shoal Creek Boulevard
Austin, TX 78757
Phone: 800-397-7633
This company publishes exclusively in the areas of psychology, special and remedial education, and speech, language, and hearing. It offers an extensive line of materials for classroom, clinical, and home use.

Recorded Books, Inc.
270 Skipjack Road
Prince Frederick, MD 20678
Phone: 800-638-1304
This company uses dedicated narrators who record books on tape that are guaranteed to be top-quality master tapes. With narrations by professional Broadway actors, the stories come to life and grab your attention!

Scansoft (Xerox Imaging Systems)
9 Centennial Drive
Peabody, MA 01960
Phone: 800-248-6550
This corporation provides its customers with the best-of-breed solutions for the organizing and editing of images that have been captured by desktop scanners and digital cameras.

Scantron Quality Computers
P. O. Box 830677
Birmingham, AL 35283-0677
Phone: 800-722-6876
This corporation provides data collection systems, survey services, and nationwide support and maintenance to education, business, and government institutions worldwide.

Scholastic
555 Broadway
New York, NY 10012-3999
Phone: 800-631-1586
This organization is a global children's publishing and media company that instills the love of reading for life-long pleasure in all children.

Seiko Instruments USA, Inc.
2990 W. Lomita Boulevard
Torrance, CA 90505
Phone: 877-344-4040
This company is responsible for the design and production of timepieces.

SoftKey, Inc.
6493 Kaiser Drive
Fremont, CA 94555
Phone: 800-227-5609
A division of Mattel, this organization is a world-wide leader in design, manufacture, and marketing of family products.

Sunburst Communications
101 Castleton Street
Pleasantville, NY 10570
Phone: 800-321-7511
This organization is a division of Houghton-Mifflin Company and is engaged in creating and publishing teaching materials.

SunSound Radio
3124 E. Roosevelt
Phoenix, AZ 85008
Phone: 602-231-0500
This organization is dedicated to providing audio access to information and knowledge normally published in a printed format.

Teacher Support Software Company
3542 NW 97th Boulevard
Gainesville, FL 32606
Phone: 904-332-6404
This company is committed to educational software that has depth and meaning for you and the students you teach.

Tech-Able
1114 Brett Drive, Suite 100
Conyers, GA 30207
Phone: 770-922-6768
This company is young and growing. It provides the best in products and services to disabled individuals in the Metro Atlanta area.

Telesensory
520 Almanar Avenue
Sunnyvale, CA 94086
Phone: 800-421-7323
This on-line organization provides innovative, technology-based products for people with low vision.

21st Century Eloquence
6782 Belvedere Road
West Palm Beach, FL 33413
Phone: 800-245-2133
This company is the provider of speech-recognition software for doctors. It specializes in high-end professional voice-recognition software solutions.

Waterloo Maple Software
57 Erb Street
W. Waterloo, Ontario
Canada N2L 6C2
Phone: 519-747-2373
This company seeks to make advanced analytical computation practical for technical professionals and students.

Wilson Learning Corp.
7500 Flying Cloud Drive
Eden Prairie, MN 55344
Phone: 800-247-7332
This corporation helps people make a connection between human development and business strategy, turning learning into performance improvement.